EVERYDAY
CLASSIC
COOKING

EVERYDAY CLASSIC
COOKING

Over 80 timeless recipes for tasty
traditional dishes

This edition first published in the United Kingdom in 2000 by Ebury Press
for WHSmith, Greenbridge Road, Swindon SN3 3LD

1 3 5 7 9 10 8 6 4 2

Ebury Press
Random House, 20 Vauxhall Bridge Road, London SW1V 2SA

Random House Australia (Pty) Limited
20 Alfred Street, Milsons Point, Sydney, New South Wales 2061, Australia

Random House New Zealand Limited
18 Poland Road, Glenfield, Auckland 10, New Zealand

Random House South Africa (Pty) Limited
Endulini, 5A Jubilee Road, Parktown 2193, South Africa

The Random House Group Limited Reg. No. 954009

www.randomhouse.co.uk

A CIP catalogue record for this book is available from the
British Library.

Editor: Cecile Landau
Recipe writers: Jacqueline Clarke; Maxine Clarke; Joanna Farrow;
Vicky Keppel-Compton; Louise Pickford; Janet Smith
Designer: Alison Shackleton
Photographers: Laurie Evans; Ken Field; Gus Filgate; Anna Hodgson;
Graham Kirk; James Murphy
Food stylists: Allyson Birch; Jacqueline Clarke; Maxine Clarke;
Joanna Farrow; Vicky Keppel-Compton; Louise Pickford; Janet Smith
Stylists: Suzy Gittins; Jane McLeish; Roisin Nield; Helen Payne; Leslie
Richardson; Helen Trent

ISBN 0 09 187884 5

Papers used by Ebury Press are natural, recyclable products made from
wood grown in sustainable forests.

Colour repro by Colourpath
Printed and bound in Italy by Milanostampa

COOKERY NOTES

● Both metric and imperial measures are given for the recipes. Follow either set of measures, but not a mixture of both as they are not interchangeable.

● All spoon measures are level unless otherwise stated. Sets of measuring spoons are available in metric and imperial for accurate measurement of small quantities.

● Ovens should be preheated to the specified temperature. Grills should also be preheated. The cooking times given in the recipes assume that this has been done.

● Use large eggs except where otherwise specified. Free-range eggs are recommended.

● Use freshly ground black pepper and sea salt unless otherwise specified.

● If stocks are required, they should be freshly made when possible. Alternatively, buy ready-made stocks or use good-quality stock cubes.

CONTENTS

INTRODUCTION

This collection of recipes is a celebration of classic cooking, though most of the recipes have been adapted to suit today's tastes and busy lifestyles. Lengthy steaming and boiling have been replaced by faster cooking methods, so that foods retain more colour and texture, and of course valuable nutrients, such as vitamins. Additional extras have been added to bring out well-loved flavours and in some cases an innovative twist has given a recipe a new lease of life.

Of course, in some cases little can be done to improve a great classic. How could we possibly interfere with a comforting Pea and Ham Soup (see page 30) or a steaming hot Steak and Kidney Pudding (see page 138), or a deep and delicious Treacle Tart (see page 174).

People are, however, more health conscious now, and so to be able to choose the 'right' foods yet still enjoy a wide range of dishes – including the occasional, slightly 'naughty', high-calorie/high-fat indulgence – we need to understand a little about basic nutrition and how to balance our diet. To help achieve this objective, follow the simple guidelines given below.

FOOD AND GOOD HEALTH

We are often told to eat healthily but are rarely told how to do so. There is no great secret to maintaining good health; we need to provide our bodies with nutrition in the form of regular amounts of protein, vitamins, minerals, fibre and carbohydrate, along with small amounts of fat.

Protein helps keep skin, teeth, internal organs and other tissues healthy, and food provides most of the body's needs. The best sources are meat, poultry, fish, eggs, dairy foods and soya.

Vitamins are necessary for many body processes and a shortage can lead to poor health. Vitamins A, B, C, D, E and K are obtained from food (although the best source of vitamin D is sunlight). Leafy vegetables and grains, among other foods, contain several different vitamins.

Minerals are required in small quantities, particularly iron, calcium and zinc. Meat and leafy green vegetables are rich in iron; calcium is found in dairy foods and oily fish, while lean meat, seafood and grains contain zinc.

Fibre is vital to a healthy digestive system. Unrefined cereals, bran, fresh vegetables and fruit all contain fibre – in fact, if you start the day with wholegrain cereal and eat plenty of fresh fruit and vegetables during the course of it, you will have enough fibre in your diet.

Carbohydrates provide energy. Sugar carbohydrates are present in fruit, milk and sugar, while potatoes, cereals, pasta, grains and pulses all contain starch carbohydrates. Starch carbohydrates should always provide a higher proportion of your energy requirements than sugar ones since they provide essential nutrients.

Fat provides heat and energy. There are three types: saturated, monounsaturated and polyunsaturated. The more saturated fat you eat, the more unhealthy, potentially, you could become. Dairy products (especially butter and cream) are high in saturated fat, as are red meats; olive oil is a monounsaturated fat while other oils, such as groundnut and corn, and oily fish are rich in polyunsaturated fat.

CREATING A BALANCED DIET

If you eat a balanced diet, your body will receive all the nutrients it needs to maintain good health and you shouldn't need vitamin and mineral supplements (unless you suffer excessive loss of certain nutrients, perhaps due to pregnancy, illness or infirmity). Avoid adding salt to cooked food; if you miss the taste, try substituting fresh herbs. If you eat some foods from each of the following categories every day, your diet will be a healthy one.

Cereals and grains such as bread, pasta, rice and breakfast cereals provide energy, fibre, B vitamins, calcium and iron.

Fruit and vegetables are a good source of vitamins, particularly A and C, and minerals, particularly iron and calcium.

Meat, poultry and fish are valuable sources of protein, energy and iron. Eat mostly white meats such as chicken, turkey and game, but balance with a little red meat once or twice a week. If possible eat fish, especially oily fish, at least twice a week.

Dairy products are good for protein, energy, calcium, minerals, vitamins D and B12, but use richer dairy foods, such as butter, eggs and cream, in moderation. Skimmed milk contains all the nutrients of whole milk without the fat.

Pulses, nuts and seeds provide protein, energy, fibre, calcium, iron and zinc.

Water helps flush out impurities in your system. Five glasses a day (including fruit juices, but not tea and coffee) will keep you healthy.

Ready-prepared foods are a great temptation, but when it comes to a healthy diet, the old adage 'fresh is best' says it all. There are very few of us who don't pop a ready meal into the microwave from time to time. So long as this is sometimes rather than often, there's no harm done, but prepared meals tend to contain high amounts of salt and should not form the basis of anyone's diet. Some takeaway foods, such as fish and chips, are high in saturated fats and are best eaten occasionally rather than often. Alternate with Indian (especially tandoori dishes), and Chinese food, which usually contain plenty of vegetables.

SHOPPING AND STORING

Good cooking is all about good shopping: buying fresh food in good condition, knowing which cuts of meat to buy, recognising when fruit and vegetables are properly ripe. Always buy the best you can afford, preferably in its natural season, when it will taste better and cost less. Often this means buying organic produce – meat, vegetables and fruit produced without using synthetic feed, pesticides or artificial fertilizers. Nearly all supermarkets now stock organic vegetables and fruit and most also sell organic chicken, eggs and other dairy products. Many greengrocers and butchers also specialise in local organic produce.

CHOOSING AND STORING MEAT

Meat should look and smell fresh. As for colour, a lurid red doesn't necessarily indicate freshness. Instead look for a good clear colour – this will darken naturally on exposure to the air. Avoid any meat with a greyish tinge or any with fat that is yellowing; fat on fresh, good quality meat should be creamy white.

Choose lean cuts as much as possible, but remember that meat should have a fair amount of marbled fat distributed throughout it. This will stop it from drying out during cooking and add flavour.

Look for poultry with a good plump breast and firm unblemished skin, and try to buy free-range or organic, if you can. Organic chicken is so much tastier than standard fresh or frozen – there is simply no comparison.

Get all meat and poultry home and into a refrigerator as soon as possible. Store it, loosely wrapped, in the coldest part and always keep raw meat and poultry well away from cooked foods to prevent cross-contamination. It is advisable to place it, freshly wrapped if appropriate, on a plate to prevent any blood dripping through the refrigerator shelves.

Remember that offal, minced meat and small cuts are best eaten on the day of purchase. Larger cuts and whole birds will keep in the refrigerator for 2–3 days. With pre-packed meat from a supermarket be guided by the use-by date. Never use meat or poultry that has even a slightly unpleasant smell, feels slimy or has a greenish tinge.

CHOOSING AND STORING FISH AND SHELLFISH

The most important thing to look for when buying fish and shellfish is freshness. The only smell coming from any fish or shellfish should resemble a whiff of sea air; any unpleasant odour indicates that it is past its best. Always buy from a reputable source with a high turnover and prepare, ideally, on the day of purchase. If you have to keep it, wrap it up well and keep in the refrigerator for no more than 24 hours.

Whole fish should have bright, clear eyes, vibrant, shiny skin and vivid pink or red gills. Fillets, steaks and cutlets should have translucent flesh and show no sign of discolouration.

When buying fresh mussels, scallops, clams or oysters in their shells, remember that they are still alive and any sign of an open shell may indicate that the specimen is far from fresh. If a sharp tap on the shell doesn't persuade the shellfish to close up, indicating that it is alive, avoid it.

Cooked shellfish, such as lobster, crab and prawns, should feel quite heavy and have a fresh sea-like aroma and intact shells.

CHOOSING AND STORING VEGETABLES AND SALADS

Look for bright, firm vegetables and crisp, fresh salad plants with a tighly packed head, where applicable. Avoid any that look shrivelled, bruised or damaged. Resist buying the largest specimens; in general the younger and smaller the vegetable, the sweeter and more tender it will be.

To enjoy them at their tastiest and most nutritious, all vegetable and salad ingredients should be eaten as soon as possible after purchase, but most will keep for a few days in a cool, dark place. Store green vegetables and salad ingredients in the salad drawer of the refrigerator. Root vegetables can be stored in a cool, dark place for up to a week. Remember that exposure to light turns potatoes green, making them poisonous.

CHOOSING AND STORING CHEESE AND EGGS

The best and most enjoyable place to buy cheese is nearly always in a specialist shop, but not everyone is lucky enough to have access to one of these. Many super-markets, however, now stock a huge variety of excellent farmhouse cheeses, so most of us have a chance to be adventurous in this area.

Buy cheese freshly cut, if you can. Remember that refrigeration dries out cheese, so don't buy too much at once. Ideally, wrap any freshly-cut cheese you wish to store in waxed paper to help keep it moist, then put it in an unsealed plastic food bag and place it in the refrigerator. Hard cheeses will keep well like this for about a week; soft cheeses will keep for 2–3 days. If your cheese was bought ready-wrapped check the use-by date. You should always remove cheese from the refrigerator 1–2 hours before serving to bring it to room temperature, as being chilled impairs its flavour.

Because of the slight risk of salmonella, always buy eggs from a reliable source with a fast turnover. This is especially important if you are using them uncooked, say in a homemade mayonnaise, or lightly cooked. Never buy cracked or damaged eggs.

Store eggs in the refrigerator with the pointed end down and check the use-by date stamped on each egg before using. Bring to room temperature before cooking.

STOCKING UP THE STORECUPBOARD

The contents of your storecupboard will depend on your personal preferences but try always to have the makings of an impromptu meal plus the basic everyday staples. Most storecupboard items will last a long time, but keep an eye on use-by dates. The following list could act as a general guideline:

• Pasta – stock a selection for quick mid-week suppers, including one long, ribbon variety, such as spaghetti and one short variety, such as penne or fusilli.

• Rice – ideally keep at least two types: long-grain and risotto rice.

• Dried pulses – form a great basis for rich casseroles and hearty soups.

• Flours and sugars – amount and variety depend on whether you bake regularly or not; once opened keep both in airtight containers.

• Baking ingredients – baking powder, dried yeast, cocoa powder, powdered gelatine, golden syrup, honey and even marzipan and food colouring are handy stock items for the keen baker.

• Dried fruits and nuts – these make nutritious snacks and add interest to many savoury and sweet dishes; always store in airtight containers when opened.

• Canned fruit and vegetables – most useful are tomatoes, pulses and sweetcorn; choose canned fruits in natural juices whenever possible.

• Canned fish – tuna, sardines and anchovies can form the backbone of many everyday meals.

• Oils and vinegars – the minimum requirement is one bland oil, such as vegetable or light olive oil, for cooking and one highly flavoured oil, such as extra-virgin olive oil, for salad dressings; wine vinegar and balsamic for dress-ings and malt vinegar for pickling and fish and chips; store all oil and vinegar away from direct heat and light.

• Flavourings and condiments – mustard, tomato ketchup, Worcestershire sauce and soy sauce are essentials; also try pesto, sun-dried tomatoes, Tabasco sauce and olive and anchovy pastes.

• Spices – cumin, coriander, turmeric, chilli powder, cinnamon, whole nutmegs, pepper, vanilla pods and vanilla and almond extracts cover most needs.

• Dried herbs – oregano, basil, sage, rosemary and thyme are worth stocking.

CLASSIC TECHNIQUES

Many of the recipes in this book use the same classic cooking techniques. The step-by-step instructions given below will help you master these skills to produce perfect results every time.

STOCK AND SAUCES

For soups, stews and gravies, a homemade stock makes a far tastier base than stock cubes, particularly if you obtain fresh bones from the butcher. If the bones are already cooked, omit the browning stage. If not required for immediate use, stock can be frozen for a later date.

MAKING STOCK

2 Transfer the bones to a large saucepan. Add a halved, unpeeled onion, 2 roughly chopped carrots, 1 halved stick of celery, 2 bay leaves, a sprinkling of black peppercorns and some fresh herbs if liked. Cover with cold water and bring slowly to the boil.

1 Put the meat bones in a roasting tin and cook in a preheated oven at 230°C/450°F/gas 8 for about 40 minutes until browned.

NOTE
For fish stock, omit the browning and use a peeled onion. Add 1–2 parsley sprigs and a strip of lemon rind and simmer for 20–30 minutes. Strain through a fine sieve.

3 Skim off any scum using a slotted spoon. Reduce the heat and simmer very gently, allowing 2 hours for chicken and poultry, 3–4 hours for red meats. Leave to cool and then strain.

MAKING WHITE SAUCE

1 Melt the butter in a saucepan. Blend in the flour and cook, stirring, for 1 minute to make a paste.

2 Remove from the heat and gradually blend in the milk until completely smooth, whisking constantly.

3 Return to a gentle heat and, whisking constantly, cook until the sauce is thickened and smooth. Add cheese, herbs (or other flavourings) and seasoning.

MAKING GRAVY

1 Using a large metal spoon, skim almost all of the fat from the roasting tin, leaving the meat juices.

2 Add a little flour to the meat juices and stir until no lumps remain.

3 Gradually pour in the stock or half stock and half wine, stirring and scraping up any residue. Slowly bring to the boil and bubble for 2–3 minutes. Season to taste.

SEARING WHOLE JOINTS

This technique is applied to meat to quickly brown and seal it before stewing and roasting.

SEARING SMALL PIECES OF MEAT

1 To sear a whole joint of meat or poultry, thoroughly pat dry using kitchen paper.

1 To sear small pieces of meat or poultry, thoroughly pat dry using kitchen paper then coat with seasoned flour.

2 Heat the oil in a frying pan. Add the joint of meat and fry on all sides, gradually turning the meat until seared evenly all over.

2 Heat the oil in the frying pan and fry off the meat in batches. Avoid adding too much to the pan in one go, otherwise it will steam rather than brown.

DEEP-FRYING

Half-fill a deep saucepan or deep-fat fryer with vegetable oil and heat to 190°C/375°F or until a piece of bread dropped in sizzles as soon as it hits the fat. Fry only a few pieces of food at a time, then drain on kitchen paper. Do not overfill the pan, otherwise the food will not cook properly.

SHALLOW-FRYING

1 Pour a little vegetable oil into a frying pan to a depth of about 5mm (¼ inch). Heat the oil to 190°C/375°F or until a piece of bread or batter sizzles as soon as it is added to the pan.

2 Add the food you wish to shallow-fry to the hot oil and cook gently, turning carefully when the food has turned golden on the underside to brown evenly all over.

SKINNING FISH

Lay the fish fillet skin-side down with the tail end towards you. Hold a filleting knife against the skin with the blade almost parallel to it, and push away from you using a sawing action.

TESTING COOKED FISH

Cooking times vary according to the thickness of the fish and the degree of heat. Test towards the end of the stated cooking time by piercing the thickest area with the tip of a fine-bladed knife. It should be just opaque.

MAKING CUSTARD

This is the recipe used to make a real, traditional custard, or crème anglaise. It also forms the basis of several desserts.

3 egg yolks
30ml (2 tbsp) caster sugar
2.5ml (½ tsp) cornflour
300ml (½ pint) milk
2.5ml (½ tsp) vanilla essence (optional)

NOTE

A traditional egg custard does not use cornflour, but you will find that adding a little to the mixture greatly reduces the risk of curdling.

VARIATION

If you prefer the taste of real vanilla use a vanilla pod instead of the essence to flavour the milk. Infuse the milk with the vanilla pod's flavour by spliting the pod, placing it in a saucepan with the milk. Then bring the milk almost to the boil and allow to simmer for 20 minutes.

2 Bring the milk to the boil in a heavy-based saucepan. Pour the milk onto the egg yolk mixture, whisking well. Return to the saucepan and add a little vanilla essence, if liked.

1 Place the egg yolks and sugar in a bowl with the cornflour and whisk until thick and creamy. Gradually whisk in a little of the milk, making sure the mixture is smooth and has no lumps.

3 Cook over the lowest possible heat, stirring constantly, for about 10 minutes until the custard thickens slightly. It should thickly coat the back of a wooden spoon. Do not boil or the custard may curdle. Strain and serve.

COOKING IN A WATER BATH

1 Stand the pâté dish, ramekins or individual pudding basins in a deep-sided roasting tin.

2 Pour boiling water into the roasting tin until it comes about a third or half-way up the sides of the dish, ramekins or pudding basins.

3 Cover completely with aluminium foil and carefully transfer the tin to the oven using oven gloves.

MAKING SUETCRUST PASTRY

1 Add the suet to the flour and stir to combine. Add enough cold water to make a slightly sticky dough.

2 After mixing with a round-bladed knife, turn the dough out onto a floured surface and knead lightly if using for pastry.

3 If shaping dumplings, divide the dough into even-sized pieces and with floured hands roll into balls.

COVERING A PIE DISH

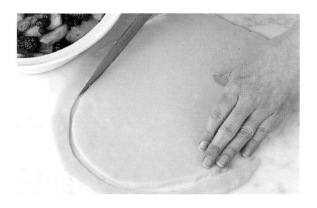

1 Roll out the pastry thinly to 5cm (2 inches) larger than the pie dish. Cut a 2.5cm (1 inch) strip from the outside.

4 Press the edges of the pastry together to seal. Using a sharp knife, trim off the excess pastry.

2 Place this strip on the moistened rim of the pie dish. Brush the pastry strip with water.

5 Knock up the edges of the pastry using a round-bladed knife to create a flaky appearance.

3 Lift the pastry lid, using the rolling pin, and place on the top of the pie dish, matching the edges of the pastry strip.

6 Gently draw the blade of the knife from the edge of the lid towards the centre. Repeat at 2.5cm (1 inch) intervals.

SOUPS

COCK-A-LEEKIE SOUP

Serves: 8
Preparation time: 20 minutes
Cooking time: 1 hour 20 minutes
Freezing: not suitable
250 cals per serving

1.4kg (3lb) oven-ready chicken

2 onions

2 carrots

2 celery sticks

1 bay leaf

900g (2lb) leeks

25g (1oz) butter

125g (4oz) ready-to-eat pitted
prunes

salt and freshly ground black
pepper

DUMPLINGS
125g (4oz) self-raising white flour

pinch of salt

50g (2oz) shredded suet

30ml (2 tbsp) chopped fresh
parsley

30ml (2 tbsp) chopped fresh
thyme

TO GARNISH
parsley and thyme sprigs

1 Peel and roughly chop the onions and carrots. Roughly chop the celery. Place the chicken in a saucepan in which it fits quite snugly. Add the chopped vegetables, bay leaf and chicken giblets (if available). Add 1.8 litres (3 pints) water. Bring to the boil, reduce the heat, cover and simmer gently for 1 hour.

2 Trim and slice the leeks. Melt the butter in a large saucepan, add the leeks and fry gently for 10 minutes. Slice the prunes.

3 Remove the chicken from the pan; strain the stock and set aside. Remove the chicken from the bones and roughly shred. Add to the stock with the prunes and leeks.

4 For the dumplings, sift the flour and salt into a bowl. Stir in the suet, herbs and about 75ml (5 tbsp) water to make a fairly firm dough. Shape the dough into 2.5cm (1 inch) balls.

5 Bring the soup just to the boil and season with salt and pepper to taste. Reduce the heat, add the dumplings and cover with a lid. Simmer for about 15–20 minutes until the dumplings are light and fluffy. Serve hot, garnished with the herbs.

TOP TIP
If possible, make the stock the day before required; allow to cool then refrigerate overnight. The next day, remove any fat from the surface.

ROASTED TOMATO SOUP

Serves: 4
Preparation time: 15 minutes
Cooking time: 50 minutes
Freezing: suitable
180 cals per serving

600g (1lb 5oz) ripe tomatoes

1 onion, peeled and cut into wedges

1 red pepper, deseeded and diced

2 garlic cloves, peeled and chopped

60ml (4 tbsp) extra-virgin olive oil

5ml (1 tsp) sugar

salt and freshly ground black pepper

30ml (2 tbsp) chopped basil leaves

300ml (½ pint) fresh chicken stock

Parmesan cheese, to serve

1 Preheat the oven to 180°C/350°F/gas 4. Skin the tomatoes by making a small cross with a sharp knife on the top of the tomato and place in a bowl. Pour over boiling water and leave for 30 seconds or until you can see the skins coming away from the flesh. Plunge the tomatoes into cold water and peel off the skin.

2 Slice the peeled tomatoes in half and place in a roasting tin with the onion wedges, diced pepper and chopped garlic. Drizzle with olive oil, add the sugar and season with salt and pepper. Roast in the oven for 45 minutes.

3 Purée the roasted vegetables and any of their cooking juices in a food processor or blender and add the handful of basil leaves. Pour the soup into a saucepan and thin by adding the stock. Check the seasoning and reheat.

4 Serve the soup with a little grated Parmesan cheese sprinkled over.

FRESH TOMATO SOUP WITH BASIL

Serves: 6
Preparation time: 20 minutes
Cooking time: 50 minutes
Freezing: suitable
90 cals per serving

30ml (2 tbsp) olive oil

1 onion, peeled and thinly sliced

2 garlic cloves, peeled and crushed

1 celery stick, thinly sliced

1 red pepper, quartered, cored and deseeded

900g (2lb) ripe plum tomatoes

900ml (1½ pints) chicken or vegetable stock

30ml (2 tbsp) sun-dried tomato paste

5ml (1 tsp) sugar

salt and freshly ground black pepper

TO SERVE
basil leaves, shredded if preferred

Parmesan cheese shavings (optional)

1 Heat the oil in a saucepan, add the onion and garlic and fry gently for about 10 minutes until soft but not browned. Add the celery and fry for a further 5 minutes.

2 Meanwhile, place the pepper on the grill rack, skin-side up, and grill until charred. Cover with a damp cloth and leave until cool, then peel away the skin and slice finely.

3 Immerse the tomatoes in a bowl of boiling water for 10 seconds, then drain and refresh under cold running water. Peel the tomatoes and roughly chop the flesh.

4 Add the tomatoes and sliced pepper to the celery and onion with the stock, sun-dried tomato paste, sugar and seasoning. Bring to the boil, cover and simmer gently for about 30 minutes.

5 Ladle the soup into warmed bowls and scatter over some basil. Top with Parmesan cheese shavings before serving if desired.

CHILLED ASPARAGUS SOUP

Serves: 6

Preparation time: 15 minutes, plus chilling

Cooking time: 40–55 minutes

Freezing: suitable

125 cals per serving

700g (1½lb) asparagus

salt and freshly ground black pepper

2 onions, peeled

25g (1oz) butter or margarine

1.4 litres (2½ pints) chicken stock

150ml (¼ pint) single cream

TO GARNISH
finely pared lemon rind

1 Cut the tips from the asparagus stalks and simmer them very gently in salted water for 3–5 minutes, until just tender. Drain well and refresh with cold water.

2 Scrape the asparagus stalks with a potato peeler or knife and cut off the woody ends; thinly slice the stalks. Chop the onions.

3 Melt the butter in a large saucepan. Add the asparagus stalks and onions, cover and cook for 5–10 minutes, until beginning to soften.

4 Add the stock and seasoning to taste. Bring to the boil, cover and simmer for 30–40 minutes, until the asparagus stalks and onions are tender.

5 Allow to cool slightly, then purée in a blender or food processor until smooth. Pass through a sieve into a bowl, then stir in the cream.

6 Chill in the refrigerator for 2–3 hours. Serve garnished with the reserved asparagus tips and finely pared lemon rind.

PEA AND HAM SOUP

Serves: 8

Preparation time: 15 minutes, plus overnight soaking

Cooking time: 1¾ hours

Freezing: suitable

340 cals per serving

450g (1lb) dried split or whole green peas

1–1.1kg (2¼–2½lb) smoked bacon knuckle

2 large onions

2 carrots

2 celery sticks

2 bay leaves

salt and freshly ground black pepper

TO SERVE
150ml (¼ pint) crème fraîche

TO GARNISH
fresh flat-leaf parsley

1 Put the dried peas in a large bowl and cover with plenty of cold water. Leave to soak overnight.

2 Place the bacon in a large saucepan and add sufficient cold water to cover. Bring slowly to the boil, then drain and return to the clean pan. Drain the peas and add to the pan.

3 Peel and roughly chop the onions. Peel and roughly slice the carrots. Cut the celery into chunks. Add to the pan with the bay leaves. Cover with cold water and bring to the boil.

4 Reduce the heat and cover with a lid. Simmer very gently for 1½ hours until the bacon and peas are very tender. Discard the bay leaves.

5 Lift the bacon from the pan. Cut into chunks, discarding the skin and bones, then chop finely.

6 Purée the soup in a blender or food processor until smooth, then place in a clean pan with the chopped meat. Heat through gently, adding a little stock if the soup is very thick. Season with a little salt if necessary, and pepper to taste.

7 Ladle the soup into warmed individual serving bowls and add a generous swirl of crème fraîche to each bowl. Serve garnished with roughly torn parsley.

TOP TIP
Use a blender in preference to a food processor for puréeing the soup as it gives a smoother result.

VARIATION
Use yellow split peas instead of green ones, cooking them in the same way.

MIXED FISH CHOWDER

Serves: 4
Preparation time: 15 minutes
Cooking time: 35–40 minutes
Freezing: not suitable
385 cals per serving

450g (1lb) smoked haddock fillet

25g (1oz) desiccated coconut

175g (6oz) onion, peeled

6 celery sticks

350g (12oz) old potatoes

1 small green pepper

50g (2oz) butter or margarine

salt and freshly ground black pepper

300ml (½ pint) milk

125g (4oz) prawns, cooked and peeled

TO GARNISH
chopped parsley or dill

1 Skin the haddock and cut into bite-sized pieces. Place the coconut in a measuring jug and make up to 300ml (½ pint) with boiling water.

2 Roughly chop the onion and celery. Peel the potatoes and cut into small chunks. Chop the green pepper, discarding the core and seeds.

3 Melt the butter in a large pan. Add the onion and celery, cover and cook for about 5 minutes until starting to soften. Add the potatoes and pepper and cook for 1–2 minutes.

4 Strain the coconut liquid and add to the pan with a further 600ml (1 pint) water. Bring to the boil, season, cover and simmer for about 20 minutes or until the vegetables are tender.

5 Add the haddock and milk to the soup. Bring to the boil, cover and simmer for 5–10 minutes, or until the fish is flaking apart. Mix in the prawns, warm gently and adjust the seasoning.

FRENCH ONION SOUP

Serves: 4
Preparation time: 20 minutes
Cooking time: 50–55 minutes
Freezing: not suitable
245 cals per serving

3 onions, peeled
50g (2oz) butter or margarine
15ml (1 tbsp) flour
900ml (1½ pints) beef stock
salt and freshly ground black pepper
1 bay leaf
½ medium French loaf
75g (3oz) Gruyère cheese, grated

1 Slice the onions thinly. Melt the butter in a saucepan, add the onions and cook gently for 15–20 minutes until dark golden brown.

2 Stir in the flour and cook, stirring, for 1 minute. Stir in the stock, seasoning and bay leaf. Bring to the boil, cover and simmer for 30 minutes.

3 Cut the loaf diagonally into 1cm (½ inch) slices and toast lightly on both sides. Place two slices in each ovenproof soup bowl. Ladle the hot soup over the bread, discarding the bay leaf.

4 Sprinkle liberally with the cheese to form a thick layer over the bread. Place under a hot grill until the cheese is melted and bubbling. Serve immediately.

MINESTRONE

Serves: 6–8
Preparation time: 30 minutes, plus overnight soaking
Cooking time: 2¾ hours
Freezing: suitable
425–320 cals per serving

175g (6oz) dried cannellini beans, soaked overnight in cold water

2 onions, peeled

2 carrots, peeled

2 celery sticks

350g (12oz) floury potatoes (such as King Edward or Maris Piper), peeled

175g (6oz) French beans

225g (8oz) dark green cabbage

60ml (4 tbsp) olive oil

3 garlic cloves, peeled and crushed

400g (14oz) can chopped tomatoes

2.3 litres (4 pints) vegetable stock or brown onion stock

125g (4oz) small pasta shapes

125g (4oz) shelled fresh or frozen peas

75ml (5 tbsp) chopped parsley

60ml (4 tbsp) pesto sauce

salt and freshly ground black pepper

TO SERVE
pesto

freshly grated Pecorino or Parmesan cheese

1 Drain the beans, put them in a very large saucepan and cover with fresh water. Bring to the boil and boil rapidly for 10 minutes, then cover and simmer for 50 minutes; drain.

2 Meanwhile prepare the vegetables. Dice the onions, carrots, celery and potatoes. Slice the French beans and roughly chop the cabbage, discarding the tough stalks.

3 Heat the oil in a large saucepan, add the onions and garlic and fry for 5–10 minutes or until golden brown. Add the carrots and celery and cook for 2 minutes.

4 Stir in the beans, tomatoes, stock, potatoes, pasta and fresh peas, if using. Bring to the boil, then reduce the heat, half-cover and simmer for 1 hour.

5 Add the frozen peas, if using, French beans, cabbage, parsley and pesto. Season with salt and pepper and simmer for 30 minutes or until the vegetables are all tender. Serve immediately, as a main course, with the pesto and cheese in separate bowls for guests to stir into their soup.

SPINACH AND POTATO SOUP

Serves: 4
Preparation time: 20 minutes
Cooking time: 40 minutes
Freezing: suitable
205 cals per serving

15ml (1 tbsp) olive oil

1 onion, peeled and chopped

2 garlic cloves, peeled and chopped

1 small red chilli, peeled and chopped

5ml (1 tsp) cumin seeds

5ml (1 tsp) garam masala

500g (1lb 2oz) potatoes, peeled and diced

500ml (18fl oz) chicken stock

200g (7oz) fresh spinach

salt and freshly ground black pepper

30ml (2 tbsp) crème fraîche

CUCUMBER RAITA
¼ cucumber, peeled, deseeded and finely chopped

30ml (2 tbsp) chopped fresh mint leaves

100ml (3½fl oz) Greek yogurt

salt and freshly ground black pepper

TO SERVE
30ml (2 tbsp) mango chutney

naan bread

1 Heat the olive oil in a large saucepan. Add the onion, garlic and chilli and cook for 10 minutes.

2 Add the cumin seeds and garam masala and cook for a further 2 minutes. Add the potatoes and stir gently to coat them.

3 Pour in the stock and bring to the boil. Cover and then cook for 20 minutes.

4 Wash and drain the spinach and add to the saucepan. Cover and cook briefly until the spinach begins to wilt.

5 Purée the soup in a food processor or blender and return to a clean saucepan to reheat. Season well with salt and pepper and then stir in the crème fraîche.

6 Make the raita by mixing the cucumber and mint leaves with the Greek yogurt. Season with salt and pepper to taste.

7 To serve, ladle the soup into warm bowls and float tablespoons of raita on top, along with a dessertspoon of mango chutney. Serve with warmed naan bread.

CREAM OF MUSHROOM SOUP

Serves: 4–6

Preparation time: 15 minutes, plus soaking

Cooking time: 35 minutes

Freezing: not suitable

285–185 cals per serving

15g (½oz) dried porcini mushrooms

150ml (¼ pint) boiling water

50g (2oz) butter

1 large onion, peeled and chopped

1 garlic clove, peeled and crushed

15ml (1 tbsp) chopped fresh sage

700g (1½lb) chestnut mushrooms, or mixed chestnut and flat mushrooms, wiped and chopped

750ml (1¼ pints) vegetable stock

150ml (¼ pint) crème fraîche

salt and freshly ground black pepper

pinch of freshly grated nutmeg

snipped chives, to garnish

1 Place the dried porcini in a bowl, pour on the boiling water and leave to soak for 20 minutes. Strain the liquid and reserve. Chop and reserve the porcini.

2 Melt half the butter in a saucepan with a tight-fitting lid, add the onion, porcini, garlic and sage and fry for 10 minutes until softened and lightly golden. Add the remaining butter, then add the mushrooms and increase the heat. Stir-fry for 5 minutes until the mushrooms are browned.

3 Stir in the reserved porcini liquid and stock. Bring to the boil, cover and simmer gently for 20 minutes. Transfer to a blender or food processor and purée until smooth. Return to the pan.

4 Stir in most of the crème fraîche and salt, pepper and nutmeg to taste, then reheat gently. Spoon into warmed bowls and add a swirl of crème fraîche and a sprinkling of snipped chives. Serve at once.

CARROT AND GINGER SOUP

Serves: 4
Preparation time: 5 minutes
Cooking time: 40 minutes
Freezing: suitable
185 cals per serving

500g (1lb 2oz) carrots, peeled and roughly chopped

250g (9oz) sweet potato, preferably the orange-fleshed variety, peeled and roughly chopped

1 onion, peeled and chopped

4cm (1½ inch) piece of ginger, peeled and chopped

25g (1oz) unsalted butter

2 garlic cloves, peeled

15ml (1 tbsp) runny honey

500ml (18fl oz) fresh chicken stock

salt and freshly ground black pepper

15ml (1tbsp) chopped chives, to garnish

1 Place the carrots, sweet potato, onion and ginger in a large saucepan with the butter, garlic and honey.

2 Dampen a large piece of greaseproof paper by screwing it up into a ball and placing it under a running tap for a few seconds. Unscrew the greaseproof paper and place it over the vegetables in the saucepan, tucking it in around the sides. Place the lid on the saucepan and cook the vegetables gently for 15 minutes.

3 Remove the greaseproof paper, add the chicken stock and season with salt and pepper to taste. Cook for a further 15 minutes.

4 Purée the soup in a food processor or blender and reheat gently. Check the seasoning and add more stock or water if necessary. Serve garnished with the chopped chives.

WINTER LENTIL SOUP

Serves: 4
Preparation time: 20 minutes
Cooking time: 30 minutes
Freezing: not suitable
450 cals per serving

225g (8oz) carrots, peeled

225g (8oz) parsnips, peeled

450g (1lb) leeks

125g (4oz) streaky bacon, derinded

30ml (2 tbsp) oil

225g (8oz) red lentils

1.7 litres (3 pints) vegetable stock

15ml (1 tbsp) tomato purée

salt and freshly ground black pepper

juice of 1 large orange

TO SERVE
grated cheese

1 Cut the carrots and parsnips into small chunks. Slice the leeks. Cut the bacon into pieces.

2 Heat the oil in a large saucepan. Add the bacon and cook until lightly browned, stirring occasionally.

3 Mix in the carrots, parsnips, leeks and lentils. Fry for 1–2 minutes, stirring occasionally.

4 Pour in the stock, adding the tomato purée and seasoning. Bring to the boil, cover and simmer for about 25 minutes or until the lentils and vegetables are tender.

5 Stir in the orange juice and adjust the seasoning. If wished, add a sprinkling of grated cheese. Serve as a main course.

STARTERS, SNACKS AND LIGHT MEALS

SMOKED MACKEREL PÂTÉ

Serves: 6
Preparation time: 15 minutes
Cooking time: nil
Freezing: suitable
195 cals per serving

275g (10oz) smoked mackerel fillets

50g (2oz) butter or margarine, softened

45ml (3 tbsp) creamed horseradish

30ml (2 tbsp) single cream

freshly ground black pepper

TO SERVE
toast or crispbreads

1 Remove the skin from the smoked mackerel and tweeze out any small bones. Flake into a bowl.

2 Add the butter, creamed horseradish and cream. Mash with a fork until evenly blended. Season with pepper; salt is not usually needed.

3 Spoon the mixture into a serving dish, cover tightly and refrigerate until required. Leave the pâté at room temperature for 30 minutes before serving. Serve with toast or crispbreads.

TOP TIP
Make sure the type of smoked mackerel you buy for this recipe does not need further cooking.

PRAWN COCKTAIL

Serves: 4
Preparation time: 10 minutes
Cooking time: nil
Freezing: not suitable
200 cals per serving

60ml (4 tbsp) mayonnaise
60ml (4 tbsp) single cream
10ml (2 tsp) tomato purée
10ml (2 tsp) lemon juice
dash of Worcestershire sauce
dash of dry sherry
salt and freshly ground black
pepper
225g (8oz) cooked peeled prawns
a few lettuce leaves, shredded
lemon slices, to garnish
thinly sliced brown bread, to serve

1 In a small bowl, mix together the mayonnaise, cream, tomato purée, lemon juice, Worcestershire sauce and sherry. Season to taste. Add the prawns and stir well to coat.

2 Place the shredded lettuce in four glasses and top with the fish mixture.

3 Garnish each prawn cocktail with lemon slices. Serve with thinly sliced brown bread.

TIGER PRAWN AND MELON SALAD

Serves: 4
Preparation time: 10 minutes
Cooking time: nil
Freezing: not suitable
170 cals per serving

½ charentais melon, skinned and diced

½ galia melon, skinned and diced

¼ cucumber, peeled, deseeded and roughly chopped

2 spring onions, sliced

125g (4oz) tiger prawns, cooked and peeled

juice and finely grated rind of 1 lime

30ml (2 tbsp) chopped fresh mint leaves

salt and freshly ground black pepper

1 Place the melon, cucumber, onions and prawns into a large bowl.

2 Add the lime juice and rind and gently stir into the melon and prawn mixture, then fold in the chopped mint. Season with salt and pepper to taste and serve at once.

DRESSED CRAB

Serves: 2–3
Preparation time: 30 minutes
Cooking time: nil
Freezing: not suitable
195–130 cals per serving

1 cooked crab, about 900g (2lb), cleaned, with the white and brown meat extracted and placed in separate bowls and the body shell left intact

salt and freshly ground black pepper

15ml (1 tbsp) lemon juice

30ml (2 tbsp) fresh white breadcrumbs

1 egg, hard-boiled

15ml (1 tbsp) chopped parsley

frisée lettuce, to serve

1 Using two forks, flake all the white meat from the crab. Season and add about 5ml (1 tsp) lemon juice.

2 Pound the brown meat in a bowl and work in the breadcrumbs with the remaining lemon juice and seasoning.

3 Using a small spoon, put the white meat in both ends of the cleaned crab shell, making sure that it is well piled up in the shell. Spoon the brown meat in a neat line down the centre between the two sections of white crab meat.

4 Chop the egg white and sieve the yolk. Hold a blunt knife between the white and brown crab meat and carefully spoon lines of parsley, sieved yolk and chopped egg white across the crab, moving the knife as you go. Serve on a bed of frisée lettuce.

CRAB SALAD

Serves: 4
Preparation time: 15 minutes
Cooking time: nil
Freezing: not suitable
260 cals per serving

150–200g (5–7oz) fresh crab meat, white and dark

2 spring onions, finely sliced

2 ripe tomatoes, deseeded and diced

juice and finely grated rind of 1 orange

small handful of fresh coriander leaves

mixed salad leaves

DRESSING:
1 red chilli, deseeded and finely chopped

1 garlic clove, peeled and finely chopped

75ml (5 tbsp) extra-virgin olive oil

salt and freshly ground black pepper

5ml (1 tsp) sugar

5ml (1 tsp) white wine vinegar

1 Break up the crab meat with your fingers into a bowl. Add the onions and tomatoes and season with salt and pepper to taste.

2 Gently stir the orange rind and coriander into the crab mixture.

3 Combine the crab mixture with the mixed salad leaves and place on individual serving plates or in a salad bowl.

4 Make the dressing by combining the chilli, garlic, and olive oil. Season with salt and pepper to taste and add the sugar. Gradually whisk in 45ml (3 tbsp) of the orange juice and the vinegar. Check for seasoning.

5 Pour the dressing over the salad and serve at once.

CREAMY LIVER PÂTÉ

Serves: 4–6

Preparation time: 40 minutes, plus chilling

Cooking time: about 50 minutes

Freezing: not suitable

1140–760 cals per serving

225g (8oz) chicken livers

225g (8oz) duck livers

2 shallots

150g (5oz) butter, softened

90ml (3fl oz) cognac, armagnac or Madeira

90ml (3fl oz) double cream or crème fraîche

salt and freshly ground black pepper

large pinch each of ground mace and allspice

warm toast, to serve

WINE JELLY

300ml (½ pint) sweet white wine, such as Sauternes

15ml (1 tbsp) powdered gelatine

ONION MARMALADE

700g (1½lb) red onions

125g (4oz) butter

120ml (4fl oz) sherry or wine vinegar

150g (5oz) caster sugar

45ml (3 tbsp) crème de cassis

300ml (½ pint) full-bodied dry red wine

1 Line a 450g (1 pint) loaf tin with cling film. Trim the chicken and duck livers, discarding any white fibrous parts and greenish discoloured bits. Peel and chop the shallots.

2 Melt 25g (1oz) butter in a frying pan, add the shallots and cook gently for 1–2 minutes until beginning to soften. Increase the heat slightly and add the livers. Turn them in the pan for 2–3 minutes until just seized but still soft and pink on the inside. Transfer to a blender.

3 Deglaze the pan with the alcohol, scraping up any sediment. Boil to reduce by half, then transfer to the blender. Add the cream, plenty of seasoning and the spices. Blend until smooth. Add the remaining softened butter and work again until smooth.

4 Pass the mixture through a fine sieve and check the seasoning. Spoon into the prepared tin and level the surface. Cool, then refrigerate for several hours or overnight, until firm.

5 Meanwhile, make the wine jelly. Pour the wine into a small pan and sprinkle over the gelatine. Stir over a low heat to dissolve, then pour into an ice cube tray and leave to set.

6 To make the onion marmalade, peel and slice the onions. Melt the butter in a pan, add the onions with the vinegar and simmer, covered, for 10 minutes until soft. Add the sugar, turn up the heat and cook, stirring, until the onions start to caramelise and the liquid has evaporated. Add the cassis and wine, and cook gently, uncovered, for 20 minutes, until all the liquid has evaporated. Season to taste.

7 To serve, turn out the terrine and cut into slices, using a warm knife. Turn out the jelly onto damp greaseproof paper and cut into cubes, using a wet knife. Serve the terrine accompanied by warm toast, the wine jelly and a spoonful of onion marmalade.

TOP TIP

Stir-fry the livers for 2–3 minutes until evenly browned but still pink and soft inside.

CHICKEN LIVERS WITH POTATO PANCAKES

Serves: 4
Preparation time: 20 minutes
Cooking time: 25–30 minutes
Freezing: suitable (for pancakes only)
335 cals per serving

PANCAKES
225g (8oz) floury potatoes

1 small egg (size 5), or ½ large egg (size 2)

30ml (2 tbsp) milk

20ml (1½ tbsp) self-raising flour

5ml (1 tsp) chopped fresh thyme

1.25ml (¼ tsp) salt

1 egg white

a little vegetable oil, for frying

SAUCE
50g (2oz) crème fraîche

15ml (1 tbsp) wholegrain mustard

7.5ml (1½ tsp) lemon juice

15ml (1 tbsp) chopped fresh chives

CHICKEN LIVERS
2 shallots

25g (1oz) butter

225g (8oz) chicken livers, thawed if frozen

salt and freshly ground black pepper

TO SERVE
50g (2oz) lamb's lettuce

extra-virgin olive oil

lemon juice, to taste

chives and lemon wedges

1 Peel the potatoes and cut into even-sized pieces. Cook in lightly salted boiling water for 12–15 minutes until tender. Drain well and mash until very smooth. Allow to cool slightly, then whisk in the egg, milk, flour, thyme and salt to form a thick smooth batter.

2 Meanwhile, make the sauce. In a bowl, mix together the crème fraîche, mustard, lemon juice and chives. Set aside to allow the flavours to develop.

3 Whisk the egg white and carefully fold into the pancake batter.

4 Preheat the oven to its lowest setting. Heat a very thin layer of oil in a frying pan. Pour in 2 large spoonfuls of the batter to form small pancakes and cook for 1–2 minutes until golden. Flip the pancakes over and cook the other side until golden. Drain on kitchen paper and keep warm in the oven. Repeat with the remaining mixture to make eight pancakes in total.

5 Peel and slice the shallots. Melt the butter in a small frying pan, add the shallots and fry gently for 5 minutes until just golden. Increase the heat, add the chicken livers and stir-fry for 3–4 minutes until the livers are well browned on the outside, but still a little pink in the centre. Season with salt and pepper to taste.

6 Toss the lamb's lettuce with a little oil and lemon juice. Arrange the potato pancakes on warmed serving plates. Sit the livers on top, scraping over any pan juices, and add a spoonful of the mustard sauce. Garnish with the salad, chives and lemon wedges.

TOP TIP
Add 2 large spoonfuls of batter to the hot oil and cook for 1–2 minutes until golden. Turn and cook the other side of the pancakes.

MUSHROOMS STUFFED WITH BACON AND CHEESE

Serves: 4
Preparation time: 20 minutes
Cooking time: 20 minutes
Freezing: not suitable
270 cals per serving

4 large cup mushrooms

45ml (3 tbsp) extra-virgin olive oil

50g (2oz) rindless smoked bacon, finely diced

2 large garlic cloves, peeled and crushed

50g (2oz) fresh white breadcrumbs

50g (2oz) ground almonds

30ml (2 tbsp) chopped fresh basil

50g (2oz) goat's cheese, diced

30ml (2 tbsp) single cream

15ml (1 tbsp) lemon juice

salt and freshly ground black pepper

basil leaves, to garnish

1 Preheat the oven the 200°C/400°F/gas 6. Cut the stalks from the mushrooms and chop them finely, reserving the whole caps.

2 Heat 30ml (2 tbsp) of the oil in a frying pan, add the mushroom caps, rounded-side down, and fry quickly for about 1 minute to brown. Remove with a slotted spoon and arrange, cup-side up, in a baking dish.

3 Add the chopped mushroom stalks, bacon and garlic to the frying pan and fry for 5 minutes, then transfer to a bowl. Add the breadcrumbs, ground almonds, basil, goat's cheese, cream, lemon juice and seasoning; mix well. Divide the stuffing between the mushroom caps.

4 Drizzle the remaining oil over the top and bake in the hot oven for 20 minutes until crisp and golden. Serve at once, garnished with basil.

MUSHROOMS ON TOAST

Serves: 4
Preparation time: 10 minutes
Cooking time: 25 minutes
Freezing: not suitable
190 cals per serving

15ml (1 tbsp) olive oil

2 shallots, peeled and chopped

4 garlic cloves, peeled and crushed

250g (9oz) chestnut mushrooms, cleaned and sliced

50g (2oz) fresh wild mushrooms, cleaned (optional)

60ml (4 tbsp) Madeira or sherry

100ml (3½fl oz) chicken or vegetable stock

salt and freshly ground black pepper

4 slices rustic bread

butter, for spreading

25g (1oz) unsalted butter, diced

30ml (2 tbsp) mixed fresh herbs, such as chives, tarragon and flat-leaf parsley

1 Warm the oil in a frying pan and add the shallots and garlic. Cook until softened and brown.

2 Add the chestnut mushrooms to the onions and garlic and cook gently for 5–10 minutes. Then add the wild mushrooms, if using, and cook gently until the juices have been absorbed. Stir from time to time, taking care not to break up the mushrooms.

3 Pour in the Madeira or sherry and gently stir, scraping up any residue on the bottom of the pan with a wooden spoon.

4 Add the stock and bring to the boil. Season to taste, turn down the heat and leave to simmer gently until you are ready to serve.

5 Meanwhile toast the bread, then butter it and place on serving plates. Just before serving, stir the diced unsalted butter into the mushrooms until it has melted and the mushrooms are glossy.

6 Scatter the chopped herbs over the buttered toast and spoon the mushroom mixture on top. Serve at once.

SMOKED HAM AND EGGS ON MUFFINS

Serves: 4
Preparation time: 5 minutes
Cooking time: about 20 minutes
Freezing: not suitable
550 cals per serving

4 white muffins

dash of vinegar

4 eggs

4 thin slices smoked ham

chervil sprigs, to garnish

SAUCE
75g (3oz) lightly salted butter

5ml (1 tsp) lemon juice

finely grated rind of ½ lemon

2 egg yolks

freshly ground black pepper

1 Preheat the oven to 150°C/300°F/gas 2. Place the muffins on a baking tray or ovenproof plate and place in the over to warm up.

2 Make the sauce. Cut the butter into small pieces. Place the lemon juice, rind and egg yolks in a heatproof bowl over a pan of simmering water. Gradually whisk in the butter until smooth. If too thick, add a little warm water. Season with pepper; keep warm.

3 Heat a saucepan of water and add the vinegar. Break the eggs into the pan and simmer gently for about 3 minutes until cooked through.

4 Meanwhile, split the warmed muffins. Arrange the bases on warmed serving plates and cover with the ham slices. Carefully lift the eggs out of the pan, drain well and place one on each serving. Spoon over the sauce and position the muffin tops. Serve garnished with chervil.

TOP TIP
If the sauce overheats and starts to curdle, add a dash of warm water and beat well. If this fails, start again with a fresh egg, gradually whisking in the curdled mixture.

CAESAR SALAD

Serves: 4
Preparation time: 15 minutes
Cooking time: 12 minutes
Freezing: not suitable
510 cals per serving

4 little gem lettuce, trimmed

85g (3oz) day-old bread

30ml (2 tbsp) olive oil

5ml (1 tsp) paprika

a pinch of cayenne pepper

25g (1oz) Parmesan cheese

DRESSING
150ml (¼ pint) light olive oil

4 garlic cloves, peeled

2 anchovy fillets in oil, drained
and chopped

1 egg yolk

15ml (1 tbsp) lemon juice

a pinch of sugar

a few drops of Worcestershire
sauce

salt and freshly ground black
pepper

1 Discard the tough outer leaves of the lettuce and separate the rest into bite-size pieces, wash briefly and shake off excess water. Transfer to a plastic bag, seal and refrigerate for 30 minutes. Remove and allow to return to room temperature.

2 Preheat the oven to 220°C/425°F/gas 7. Cut the stale bread into cubes, then combine the oil, paprika and cayenne and toss with the bread. Spread out on a baking sheet and roast in the hot oven for 6–8 minutes until crisp and golden. Set aside.

3 Prepare the dressing. Place the oil in a small saucepan, add the garlic and anchovies and heat gently for 5–6 minutes until soft and golden. Leave on one side until cold, then strain and reserve the oil.

4 Mash the garlic cloves and anchovy to form a paste and place in a bowl with the egg yolk, lemon juice, sugar and Worcestershire sauce. Beat until pale and then gradually whisk in the reserved oil in a steady stream until the mixture thickens.

5 Place the lettuce leaves in a large bowl and scatter over the croûtons. Finely grate the Parmesan cheese over the top. Pour over the dressing and toss well until all the leaves and croutons are well coated. Serve immediately.

TOP TIP
Thin the dressing with a little boiling water if necessary.

SPINACH AND BACON SALAD

Serves: 6
Preparation time: 15 minutes
Cooking time: 15 minutes
Freezing: not suitable
615 cals per serving

4 slices rustic bread

30ml (2 tbsp) extra-virgin olive oil

15ml (1 tbsp) sun-dried tomato oil
(reserved from tomatoes used for
dressing)

25g (1oz) freshly grated Parmesan
cheese

25g (1oz) pinenuts

225g (8oz) bacon, cut into 5mm
(¼ inch) cubes

450g (1lb) baby spinach leaves,
cleaned

225g (8oz) cherry tomatoes,
halved

TOMATO AND OLIVE DRESSING
4 sun-dried tomatoes in oil

85g (3oz) black olives, stoned and
roughly chopped

15ml (1 tbsp) capers, drained and
roughly chopped

2 garlic cloves, peeled and roughly
chopped

15ml (1 tbsp) roughly chopped
fresh flat-leaf parsley

15ml (1tbsp) roughly chopped
fresh basil leaves

60ml (4 tbsp) extra-virgin olive oil

10ml (2 tsp) lemon juice

salt and freshly ground black
pepper

1 First make the dressing. Drain the sundried tomatoes reserving the oil. Roughly chop the tomatoes and place in a bowl with the olives, capers, garlic, parsley and basil. Stir in the olive oil and lemon juice and season with salt and pepper to taste.

2 Preheat the oven to 200°C/400°F/gas 6. Cut and tear the bread into large chunks and place on a baking sheet. Dribble the olive oil and sun-dried tomato oil over the bread and scatter the Parmesan and pinenuts on top. Bake in the oven for 5–10 minutes until crisp and golden. Remove from the oven and, when cool enough to handle, break up into small pieces and put to one side.

3 Just before serving, preheat the grill and cook the bacon pieces until brown and crispy.

4 In a large salad bowl, toss the spinach leaves with the cherry tomatoes. Add the broken-up pieces of Parmesan-topped baked bread and the warm crispy bacon, then quickly stir in the dressing and serve at once.

CREAMY LEEK TART

Serves: 6

Preparation time: 30 minutes, plus chilling

Cooking time: 35–40 minutes

Freezing: not suitable

640 cals per serving

PASTRY

250g (9oz) plain white flour

5ml (1 tsp) salt

125g (4½oz) butter, softened

1 large egg yolk (size 1)

FILLING

1.4kg (3lb) leeks, trimmed

50g (2oz) butter

salt and freshly ground black pepper

3 egg yolks

freshly grated nutmeg

300ml (½ pint) crème fraîche or double cream

1 To make the pastry, sift the flour and salt onto a sheet of greaseproof paper. Put the butter and egg yolk in a food processor and blend until smooth. Shoot in the flour and work until just combined. Turn out onto a lightly floured work surface and knead gently until smooth. Form into a ball, flatten and wrap in cling film. Chill in the refrigerator for at least 30 minutes. Allow to come to room temperature before rolling out.

2 Meanwhile, prepare the filling. Slice or chop the leeks. Melt the butter in a large saucepan, add the leeks and stir to coat in the butter. Add 30ml (2 tbsp) water, cover and cook gently, stirring occasionally, for about 20 minutes until very soft, but not coloured. Season well. Set aside to cool.

3 Preheat the oven to 200°C/400°F/gas 6. Roll out the pastry thinly on a lightly floured surface and use to line a 25cm (10 inch) loose-bottomed flan tin. Chill for 20 minutes, then lightly prick the base with a fork.

4 Beat the egg yolks and cream together, adding a little freshly grated nutmeg. Spread the leeks in the pastry case and pour over the egg and cream mixture.

5 Bake in the oven for 15 minutes, then lower the oven setting to 190°C/375°F/gas 5 and bake for a further 20–25 minutes until set and browned on top. Serve warm or cold.

VARIATIONS
- *Add 125g (4oz) chopped Parma ham or jambon cru du pays to the filling at stage 4.*
- *Sprinkle 125g (4oz) grated Gruyère over the top of the flan before cooking.*

FOUR CHEESE AND TOMATO PIZZA

Serves: 4

Preparation time: 30 minutes, plus rising

Cooking time: 10–15 minutes

Freezing: suitable

690 cals per serving

PIZZA DOUGH

225g (8oz) strong plain white flour

2.5ml (½ tsp) salt

2.5ml (½ tsp) easy-blend dried yeast

150ml (¼ pint) warm water

15ml (1 tbsp) extra-virgin olive oil

TOPPING

50g (2oz) drained sun-dried tomatoes in oil, sliced

125g (4oz) mozzarella cheese, grated

125g (4oz) dolcelatte cheese, diced

125g (4oz) mascarpone cheese

50g (2oz) Parmesan cheese, freshly grated

5ml (1tsp) dried oregano

salt and freshly ground black pepper

1 First make the the pizza dough. Sift the flour and salt into a bowl and stir in the yeast. Make a well in the centre and gradually work in the water and oil to form a soft dough.

2 Knead the dough on a lightly floured surface for 8–10 minutes until smooth and elastic. Place in an oiled bowl, cover with oiled cling film and leave to rise in a warm place for about 1 hour or until doubled in size.

3 Preheat a large baking sheet on the top shelf of the oven at 230°C/450°F/gas 8. Knock back the risen dough and divide into four equal pieces.

4 On a well floured board, roll out each piece of dough to a thin 18cm (7 inch) round. Top with the sun-dried tomatoes and cheeses, then sprinkle with the oregano and seasoning.

5 Carefully transfer the pizzas to the hot baking sheet and bake in the preheated oven for 10–15 minutes until bubbling and golden. Serve at once.

TOP TIP

If you haven't got a baking sheet large enough to take all four pizzas at once, bake the pizzas in two batches.

CHEESE AND ONION TART

Serves: 6–8

Preparation time: 25 minutes, plus chilling

Cooking time: 45 minutes

Freezing: suitable

585–435 cals per serving

PASTRY

225g (8oz) plain flour

two good pinches of salt

7ml (1 heaped tsp) dry English mustard

125g (4oz) unsalted butter, cut into 1.25cm (½ inch) cubes

1 egg yolk

30ml (2 tbsp) milk

FILLING

15ml (1 tbsp) olive oil

1 red onion, peeled and finely chopped

225g (8oz) cream cheese

150ml (¼ pint) double cream

4 eggs

salt and freshly ground black pepper

2.5ml (½ tsp) freshly grated nutmeg

175g (6oz) mature Cheddar cheese, grated

15ml (1 tbsp) chopped chives

1 Preheat the oven to 200°C/400°F/gas 6. Make the shortcrust pastry by sifting together the flour, salt and mustard into a food processor bowl. Add the butter and process until the mixture resembles fine breadcrumbs. Combine the egg yolk with the milk and pour through the feeder of the food processor. Process until the pastry forms a ball. Add more milk if required.

2 Roll out the pastry on a floured surface and use to line a 25cm (10 inch) flan case. Line the pastry case with crumpled foil and bake blind in the preheated oven for 10 minutes. Remove the foil and return to the oven for a further 5 minutes. Remove the pastry case and reduce the oven temperature to 180°C/350°F/gas 4.

3 Prepare the filling. Warm the olive oil in a frying pan and add the onion. Cook until soft, transparent and just turning brown. Remove from the pan and place in the cooked pastry case.

4 Beat the cream cheese with the cream in a large bowl. Add the eggs and season with salt and pepper. Add the nutmeg and whisk until mixed. Stir the Cheddar cheese and chives into the mixture. Pour into the pastry case on top of the onions.

5 Cook the tart in the preheated oven for 20 minutes or until the filling is set. Allow the tart to rest for at least 5 minutes if serving hot, or serve cold.

CHEESE AND APPLE PARCELS

Makes: 10

Preparation time: 35 minutes, plus chilling

Cooking time: about 15 minutes

Freezing: suitable (at stage 5)

260 cals per parcel

PASTRY

175g (6oz) firm unsalted butter

225g (8oz) plain white flour

pinch of salt

5ml (1 tsp) lemon juice

FILLING

125g (4oz) Cheshire cheese

1 large dessert apple

45ml (3 tbsp) chopped fresh parsley

salt and freshly ground black pepper

beaten egg, to glaze

TO SERVE

salad leaves

1 To make the pastry, cut the butter into small dice. Sift the flour and salt into a bowl. Add the butter, lemon juice and 100ml (3½fl oz) very cold water. Using a round-bladed knife, mix to a soft dough, adding a little extra water if the mixture is too dry.

2 Knead lightly, then roll out to an oblong, about 30cm (12 inches) long and 10cm (4 inches) wide on a lightly-floured surface. Fold the bottom third up and the lower third down, keeping the edges straight, then give the pastry a quarter turn. Repeat the rolling, folding and turning four more times. Wrap in greaseproof paper and leave to rest in the refrigerator for at least 30 minutes.

3 For the filling, crumble the cheese into a bowl. Peel, core and quarter the apple, then cut into small dice. Add to the bowl with the parsley and seasoning.

4 Preheat the oven to 220°C/425°F/gas 7. Roll out half the pastry thinly on a lightly floured surface and cut out five 12cm (5 inch) rounds, using a small saucer or bowl as a guide.

5 Brush the edges of the circles with beaten egg, then spoon a little filling onto one side of each of the rounds. Fold the other half over the filling and press the edges together well to seal. Lightly flute the edges.

6 Transfer the pastries to a lightly greased baking sheet and brush with beaten egg. Score each pastry several times across the top. Use the remaining pastry and filling to make five more parcels in the same way. Bake in the preheated oven for about 15 minutes until risen and golden. Serve warm with a lightly dressed salad.

SMOKED HADDOCK AND EGG PANCAKES

Serves: 3–4
Preparation time: 30 minutes
Cooking time: 20 minutes
Freezing: not suitable
720–540 cals per serving

350g (12oz) smoked haddock fillet

2 eggs

40g (1½oz) butter or margarine

25g (1oz) plain flour

200ml (7fl oz) milk

150ml (¼ pint) soured cream

15ml (1 tbsp) snipped chives

freshly ground black pepper

6 pancakes

50g (2oz) fresh brown
breadcrumbs

1 Preheat the oven to 190°C/375°F/gas 5. Poach the fish in enough water to cover for about 5–7 minutes until tender. Drain, skin and flake into large pieces, removing any bones. Hardboil the eggs for 7 minutes, then shell and chop roughly.

2 Melt 25g (1oz) butter in a saucepan, add the flour and cook, stirring, for 1 minute. Remove from the heat and gradually stir in the milk and soured cream. Bring to the boil, stirring constantly, then lower the heat and cook gently, stirring, for 2–3 minutes.

3 Add the flaked fish and roughly chopped eggs to the sauce. Stir in the chives and season with plenty of black pepper; the fish adds sufficient salt. Divide the mixture among the prepared pancakes and roll up.

4 Place in a shallow ovenproof dish and sprinkle with the breadcrumbs. Melt the remaining butter and drizzle over the top. Bake in the preheated oven for about 20 minutes or until bubbling and thoroughly heated through.

MACARONI CHEESE

Serves: 4
Preparation time: 10 minutes
Cooking time: 35–40 minutes
Freezing: not suitable
790 cals per serving

225g (8oz) short-cut macaroni or small pasta shapes

salt and freshly ground black pepper

65g (2½oz) butter or margarine

65g (2½oz) plain flour

900ml (1½ pints) milk

pinch of freshly grated nutmeg or 2.5ml (½ tsp) mustard

225g (8oz) mature Cheddar cheese, grated

45ml (3 tbsp) fresh wholemeal breadcrumbs

parsley sprigs, to garnish

1 Preheat the oven to 200°C/400°F/gas 6. Cook the macaroni in boiling salted water for about 10 minutes or until just tender. Drain well.

2 Meanwhile, melt the butter in a saucepan, stir in the flour and cook gently for 1 minute. Remove from the heat and gradually stir in the milk. Bring to the boil and cook, stirring, until the sauce thickens.

3 Remove from the heat, season with salt and pepper and add the nutmeg or mustard, most of the cheese and the macaroni. Pour into an ovenproof dish.

4 Sprinkle with the remaining cheese and the breadcrumbs. Brown under a hot grill or place on a baking sheet and bake in the preheated oven for 25–30 minutes or until golden and bubbling. Serve immediately, garnished with parsley.

VARIATION

Cauliflower cheese: Omit the macaroni. Trim one large cauliflower and cut into florets (you will need about 800g/1¾lb florets). Cook the cauliflower florets in fast boiling salted water for about 10 minutes or until just tender, then drain thoroughly. Place in an ovenproof dish. Pour the cheese sauce over the cauliflower. Sprinkle with the remaining cheese and breadcrumbs and grill or bake as above.

CLASSIC OMELETTE

Serves: 1
Preparation time: 5 minutes
Cooking time: 1–1½ minutes
Freezing: not suitable
390 cals per serving

2–3 eggs

salt and freshly ground black pepper

15ml (1 tbsp) milk or water

butter or margarine for frying

salad and warm bread, to serve

1 Whisk the eggs just enough to break them down; over-beating spoils the texture of the omelette. Season with salt and pepper and add the milk or water.

2 Place an omelette pan or non-stick frying pan over a gentle heat. When it is hot add a generous knob of butter and heat until it is foaming but not brown.

3 Add the beaten eggs. Stir gently with a fork or wooden spatula, drawing the mixture from the sides to the centre as it sets and letting the liquid egg in the centre run to the sides. When the eggs have set, stop stirring and cook for a further 30 seconds–1 minute until the omelette is golden brown underneath and still creamy on top. Don't over-cook or it will be tough. Serve at once, with a salad and warm bread.

VARIATIONS
You can fill the omelette with any filling of your choice. It is best to stick to something simple, such as grated cheese, chopped ham or lightly cooked mushrooms or tomatoes. Add the filling as soon as the omelette is cooked, at the end of stage 3. Then tilt the pan away from you slightly and use a palette knife to fold a third of the omelette over the filling to the centre, then fold over the opposite third. Slide the omelette out on to a warmed plate, letting it flip over so that the folded sides are underneath.

CHEESE SOUFFLÉ

Serves: 4

Preparation time: 20 minutes, plus standing

Cooking time: 30 minutes

Freezing: not suitable

295 cals per serving

15ml (1 tbsp) freshly grated Parmesan cheese

200ml (7fl oz) milk

few onion and carrot slices

1 bay leaf

6 black peppercorns

25g (1oz) butter or margarine

30ml (2 tbsp) plain flour

10ml (2 tsp) Dijon mustard

salt and freshly ground black pepper

cayenne pepper

4 eggs, separated, plus 1 egg white

75g (3oz) mature Cheddar cheese, finely grated

1 Grease a 1.3 litre (2¼ pint) soufflé dish with butter. Sprinkle the Parmesan into the dish and tilt the dish, knocking the sides gently until they are evenly coated with cheese. Put the milk in a saucepan with the onion and carrot slices, bay leaf and peppercorns. Bring slowly to the boil, remove from the heat, cover and leave to infuse for 30 minutes; strain.

2 Melt the butter in a saucepan and stir in the flour and mustard. Season with salt, pepper and cayenne, and cook for 1 minute, stirring. Remove from the heat and gradually stir in the milk. Bring to the boil slowly and cook, stirring, until the sauce thickens. Cool a little, then beat in the egg yolks, one at a time. Sprinkle the Cheddar cheese over the sauce, reserving 15ml (1 tbsp) for the topping.

3 Stir the cheese into the sauce until evenly blended. Using a hand or electric mixer, whisk the egg whites until they stand in soft peaks.

4 Mix one large spoonful of egg white into the sauce to lighten it. Gently pour the sauce over the remaining egg whites and carefully fold the ingredients together, using a metal spoon; do not overmix.

5 Pour the soufflé mixture gently into the prepared dish; it should come about three-quarters of the way up the side of the dish.

6 Sprinkle with the reserved cheese and run a knife around the edge of the mixture. Stand the dish on a baking sheet and bake at 180°C/350°F/gas 4 for about 30 minutes, until golden brown on the top, well risen and just firm to the touch. Serve immediately.

TOP TIP

Use a proper straight-sided soufflé dish to get the best rise. Running a knife around the edge of the mixture before it goes into the oven helps to achieve the classic hat effect. If necessary, the soufflé can be prepared ahead to the end of stage 2 and left to stand for several hours before completing.

VARIATIONS

• *Replace the Cheddar cheese with a semi-hard blue cheese, such as Stilton.*

• *Omit the cheese and instead flavour the soufflé with smoked haddock. Add 75g (3oz) finely flaked smoked haddock to the sauce until evenly blended at the beginning of stage 3.*

FISH AND SHELLFISH

TROUT WITH CRISPY BACON AND ALMOND SAUCE

Serves: 4
Preparation time: 15 minutes
Cooking time: about 10 minutes
Freezing: not suitable
660 cals per serving

4 small whole trout, gutted

8 thin rashers smoked streaky bacon

25g (1oz) butter

30ml (2 tbsp) oil

25g (1oz) slivered almonds, toasted

parsley sprigs, to garnish

SAUCE
½ small leek (green end)

25g (1oz) butter

2 garlic cloves, peeled and crushed

25g (1oz) ground almonds

60ml (4 tbsp) ginger wine

45ml (3 tbsp) double cream

salt and freshly ground black pepper

1 Lightly score the fish once or twice on each side. Wrap two rashers of bacon around each fish, securing in place with wooden cocktail sticks.

2 Melt the butter with the oil in a frying pan. Add the trout and fry gently for 5 minutes until the bacon is crisp and golden. Turn and fry for a further 5 minutes or until cooked through. Scatter the slivered almonds over the trout.

3 Meanwhile, trim and thinly slice the leek. Melt the butter in a saucepan. Add the leek and garlic and fry for 5 minutes until the leeks are softened.

4 Stir in the ground almonds and ginger wine and cook gently for 3 minutes until the mixture forms a soft paste. Stir in the cream and season with salt and pepper to taste.

5 Arrange the trout and almonds on warmed serving plates and add a generous spoonful of the sauce. Serve garnished with parsley.

TOP TIP
If short of space in the frying pan, cut off the fish heads before frying.

VARIATION
Use a medium sweet wine instead of the ginger wine.

BAKED HERRINGS WITH MUSHROOM AND OATMEAL STUFFING

Serves: 4
Preparation time: 20 minutes
Cooking time: 15–20 minutes
Freezing: not suitable
500 cals per serving

1 small onion

15ml (1 tbsp) sunflower oil

125g (4oz) brown cap mushrooms

30ml (2 tbsp) oatmeal

45ml (3 tbsp) chopped fresh parsley

juice of ½ lemon

salt and freshly ground black pepper

1 egg yolk

25g (1oz) butter

4 herrings, each about 300g (10oz), cleaned

lemon wedges, to serve

1 Preheat the oven to 190°F/375°F/gas 5. Peel and finely chop the onion. Heat the oil in a pan, add the onion and cook for about 5 minutes until softened. Meanwhile, roughly chop the mushrooms.

2 Add the oatmeal to the onion and cook, stirring, for a further 3–4 minutes, until the oatmeal turns slightly golden.

3 Remove from the heat and stir in the mushrooms, parsley and lemon juice. Season with salt and pepper to taste. Stir in the egg yolk to bind the mixture together.

4 Use a little of the butter to grease an ovenproof dish. Divide the stuffing between the herring, filling the cavities. Lay the fish in the prepared dish and dot with the remaining butter. Cover and bake for 10 minutes. Uncover and cook for a further 5–8 minutes, until the fish flakes easily. Serve immediately.

VARIATION
Use the stuffing to fill mackerel instead of herring. Increase the baking time by about 5 minutes.

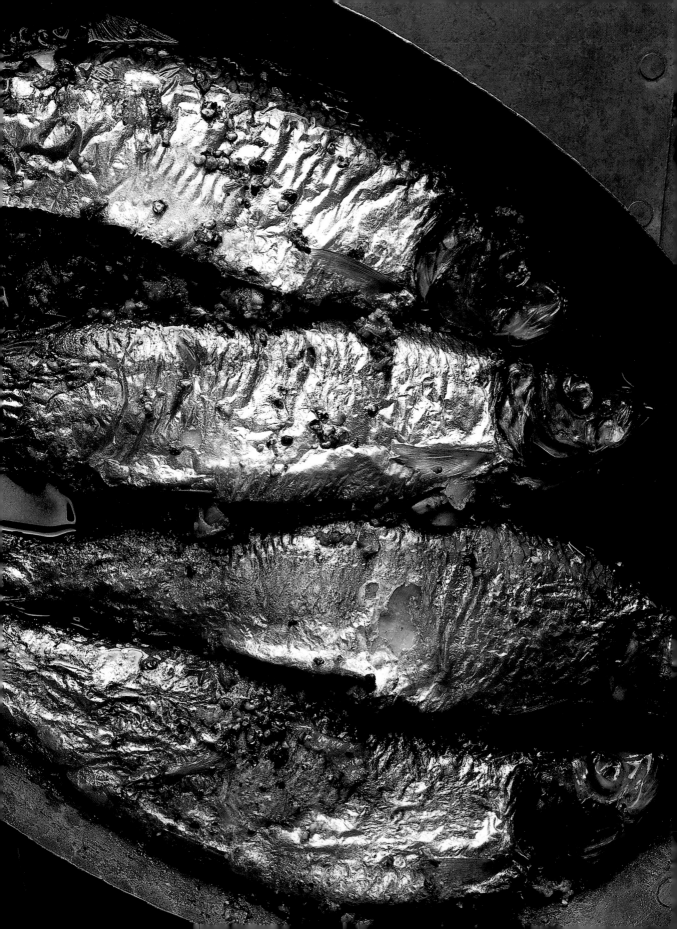

FISH CAKES WITH HERBS

Serves: 4

Preparation time: 15 minutes

Cooking time: 10 minutes

Freezing: not suitable

175 cals per serving

275g (10oz) haddock fillet, skinned

15ml (1 tbsp) lemon juice

15ml (1 tbsp) Worcestershire sauce

15ml (1 tbsp) creamed horseradish

100ml (4fl oz) milk

15ml (1 tbsp) snipped chives

15ml (1 tbsp) chopped parsley

350g (12oz) cooked potatoes, mashed

50g (2oz) fresh wholemeal breadcrumbs

1 Preheat the grill to a moderate heat. Purée the fish in a blender or food processor with the lemon juice, Worcestershire sauce and horseradish. Transfer to a bowl and stir in the milk, herbs and potatoes until evenly blended.

2 Spread the breadcrumbs out on a plate. Shape the mixture into four fish cakes and dip into the breadcrumbs to coat evenly.

3 Grill under the hot grill for 5 minutes on each side, until browned. Serve with a green salad.

SALMON FILLETS WITH CHERVIL SAUCE

Serves: 6
Preparation time: 20 minutes
Cooking time: about 20 minutes
Freezing: not suitable
500 cals per serving

3 salmon tail fillets, each
weighing about 300g (10oz)

1 fennel bulb

25g (1oz) butter

1 lemon

20ml (4 tsp) capers

30ml (2 tbsp) roughly chopped
fresh chervil

salt and freshly ground black
pepper

fresh chervil sprigs, to garnish

CHERVIL SAUCE
2.5ml (½ tsp) cornflour

1 egg yolk

250ml (8fl oz) double cream

grated rind of 1 lemon

30ml (2 tbsp) lemon juice

45ml (3 tbsp) roughly chopped
fresh chervil

1 First make the sauce. Blend the cornflour with a little water in a small saucepan until smooth. Stir in the egg yolk, cream, lemon rind and juice, chervil, and pepper to taste. Set aside.

2 Remove the skin from the salmon fillets and halve each fillet lengthways. Trim and thinly slice the fennel. Melt 15g (½oz) of the butter in a frying pan. Add the fennel and fry gently for 3 minutes to soften. Cool slightly.

3 Preheat the oven to 200°C/400°F/gas 6. Cut out six 25cm (10 inch) circles of greaseproof paper. Spread each circle to within 2.5cm (1 inch) of the edge with the remaining butter. Position a piece of salmon to one side of each circle.

4 Arrange a little fennel on each salmon fillet. Pare strips of lemon rind with a zester and scatter over the fish with the capers, chervil and seasoning.

5 Fold the paper over the filling and twist the edges together to seal completely. Place on a large baking sheet and bake for 20 minutes.

6 Slit one fish parcel open in the centre to test whether the salmon is cooked. Pierce the thickest part of the salmon with a knife; if cooked, the flesh should have turned opaque. Return the fish parcels to the oven for a little longer if necessary.

7 Gently heat the sauce until slightly thickened. Split the top of each parcel open with a knife and garnish with sprigs of chervil. Serve with the chervil sauce.

VARIATION
Other small fish fillets, such as cod and haddock, or fish steaks can be cooked in the same way.

COD IN CRISP BATTER WITH LEMON AND PARSLEY SAUCE

Serves: 4
Preparation time: 15 minutes, plus standing
Cooking time: about 15 minutes
Freezing: not suitable
655 cals per serving

700g (1½lb) cod or haddock fillet

30ml (2 tbsp) plain flour

salt and freshly ground black pepper

oil for deep-drying

lemon wedges, to garnish

BATTER
200g (7oz) self-raising flour

2.5ml (½ tsp) baking powder

2.5ml (½ tsp) salt

SAUCE
25g (1oz) butter

15ml (1 tbsp) milk

60ml (4 tbsp) chopped fresh parsley

finely grated rind of 1 lemon

juice of ½ lemon

45ml (3 tbsp) double cream

1 First make the batter. Sift the flour, baking powder and salt into a bowl. Gradually whisk in 300ml (½ pint) water to make a smooth batter. Leave to stand for 30 minutes–1 hour.

2 Skin the fish if necessary and remove any small bones. Cut the fillets into slightly smaller pieces. Season the flour with salt and pepper and use to coat the fish pieces evenly.

3 To make the sauce, melt the butter in a small saucepan. Add the flour and cook, stirring, for 1 minute. Remove from the heat and gradually blend in the milk. Return to the heat and cook gently, stirring, until thickened. Stir in the parsley, lemon rind and juice, cream and seasoning.

4 Half fill a large deep saucepan or deep-fat fryer with oil and heat to 190°C/375°F or until a a small piece of bread dropped in sizzles immediately (remove the bread before cooking the fish). Cook the fish pieces in three batches. Coat them in the batter, lower into the oil and deep-fry for about 5 minutes until golden and crisp.

5 Lift the fish out with a slotted spoon and drain on kitchen paper. Keep warm while frying the remainder.

6 Meanwhile, gently reheat the sauce. Place the fish on warmed serving plates and garnish with lemon wedges. Serve with the lemon and parsley sauce, and vegetables of your choice.

TOP TIP
It is worth making chips to serve with the fish while you're using the deep-fat fryer. Peel and cut the potatoes into chips. Put into the frying basket and lower into the oil. Deep-fry at 200°C/400°F for 6–7 minutes until starting to colour. Lift the basket and drain the chips, then deep-fry for a further 3 minutes until golden and crisp. Drain, season and keep warm while frying the fish.

CHUNKY COD CROQUE MONSIEUR

Serves: 4
Preparation time: 10 minutes
Cooking time: 20 minutes
Freezing: not suitable
800 cals per serving

125g (4oz) Gruyère cheese

5ml (1 tsp) dry mustard powder

15ml (1 tbsp) chopped chives

salt and freshly ground black pepper

150ml (¼ pint) crème fraîche, or enough to form a paste

4 slices Parma ham

4 pieces skinless chunky cod fillet, each weighing about 150g (5oz)

1 Preheat the oven to 200°C/400°F/gas 6. Make up the cheese topping by grating the Gruyère cheese into a bowl and adding the dry mustard powder, chopped chives, seasonings and enough crème fraîche to make a paste.

2 Wrap a slice of Parma ham around each cod fillet. Grease the bottom of an ovenproof dish and lay the cod in the bottom. Spread the cheese topping over the fish.

3 Bake in the preheated oven for 20 minutes or until golden and bubbling. Serve immediately.

BAKED COD WITH POTATOES

Serves: 4
Preparation time: 10 minutes
Cooking time: 1 hour
Freezing: not suitable
395 cals per serving

750g (1½lb) potatoes

1 onion

75g (3oz) butter

salt and freshly ground black pepper

a few fresh thyme sprigs

300ml (½ pint) chicken stock

4 thick cod fillets, each about 150g (5oz)

snipped fresh chives, to garnish

1 Preheat the oven to 190°C/375°F/gas 5. Peel the potatoes and onion, then slice thinly and as evenly as possible.

2 Use 25g (1oz) of the butter to grease an ovenproof dish. Layer the potatoes and onion alternately in the dish, sprinkling each layer with salt, pepper and thyme. Dot with half of the remaining butter. Pour in the stock and bake in the preheated oven for 40–50 minutes.

3 Melt the remaining butter in a non-stick frying pan, add the cod fillets and fry briefly until golden on both sides.

4 Place the fish on top of the potatoes. Cover the dish and return to the oven for a further 10–15 minutes. The fish should be firm but tender; check by prising the flesh away from the bone – if it comes away quite easily, the fish is ready.

5 Sprinkle the dish with the chives and serve immediately.

VARIATION
Use haddock, sole or whiting instead of cod.

COD IN CIDER AND ORANGE SAUCE

Serves: 4
Preparation time: 15 minutes
Cooking time: 25–30 minutes
Freezing: suitable
160 cals per serving

4 cod fillets, skinned, each weighing about 175g (6oz)

1 orange

175g (6oz) onion, peeled and chopped

freshly ground black pepper

150ml (5fl oz) medium-dry cider

125ml (4fl oz) fish stock

10ml (2 tsp) chopped fresh coriander

fresh coriander sprigs and orange slices, to garnish

1 Preheat the oven to 190°C/375°F/gas 5. Place the fish in a 1.1 litre (2 pint) ovenproof dish. Pare the rind from the orange and cut into 7.5cm (3 inch) long thin strips. Place on top of the fish with the onion and season with pepper.

2 Mix 30ml (2 tbsp) orange juice with the cider and fish stock. Pour over the fish, cover and bake in the preheated oven for 20–25 minutes or until the fish is cooked through.

3 Carefully place the onion, orange strips and fish in a serving dish and keep them warm.

4 Strain the cooking liquid into a small saucepan and boil rapidly for about 5 minutes or until the liquid is reduced by half. Pour over the fish and sprinkle with the coriander. Garnish with coriander sprigs and orange slices and serve immediately.

SKATE WITH A CREAMY CAPER SAUCE

Serves: 4
Preparation time: 5 minutes
Cooking time: 15–20 minutes
Freezing: not suitable
330 cals per serving

4 pieces of skate wing, each weighing about 200g (7oz)

2 shallots

1 celery stick

2 bay leaves

5ml (1 tsp) black peppercorns

75ml (5 tbsp) cider vinegar

10ml (2 tsp) capers

150ml (¼ pint) double cream

30ml (2 tbsp) chopped fresh parsley

salt and freshly ground black pepper

fresh parsley sprigs, to garnish

1 Ask your fishmonger to skin the skate wings if necessary, and cut to the right portion size.

2 Peel and roughly chop the shallots. Break the celery stick into three or four pieces. Put these into a large saucepan with the bay leaves, black peppercorns and 60 ml (4 tbsp) of the cider vinegar. Add 1.2 litres (2 pints) cold water, slide in the skate and slowly bring to just below the boil – the surface should barely bubble.

3 Cover the pan, lower the heat and cook for 7–10 minutes, until the skate flesh just parts from the central cartilaginous layer.

4 While the fish is cooking, chop the capers and put them into a small pan with the cream. Stir in the parsley and season with salt and pepper. Bring to the boil, lower the heat and simmer for 1 minute. Take off the heat and stir in the remaining 15ml (1 tbsp) vinegar. Check the seasoning.

5 Lift the skate from the poaching liquor on to warmed serving plates. Spoon on the cream sauce and garnish with parsley sprigs. Serve immediately, accompanied by boiled new potatoes and a green vegetable.

TOP TIP
Drain the skate scrupulously as you lift it from the poaching liquor and flick off any flavouring debris adhering to the fish.

GOLDEN CRUMBED PLAICE

Serves: 4
Preparation time: 15 minutes
Cooking time: 10 minutes
Freezing: not suitable
268 cals per serving

450g (1lb) fillet of plaice, skinned

dash of lemon juice

1 bay leaf

salt and freshly ground black pepper

40g (1½oz) butter

50g (2oz) fresh brown breadcrumbs

3 sticks celery, roughly chopped

25g (1oz) chopped walnuts

30ml (2 tbsp) chopped fresh parsley

fresh parsley sprigs, to garnish

grilled tomato slices, to serve

1 If necessary, divide each fish fillet in half, then roll up, the skinned sides inside; secure with a cocktail stick.

2 Place the fish in a frying pan and barely cover with water. Add the lemon juice, bay leaf and seasoning. Cover and simmer for about 5 minutes until tender.

3 Meanwhile, melt the butter in a frying pan. Add the crumbs and fry, stirring occasionally, until they are beginning to brown. Mix in the celery and walnuts and cook until the crumbs are golden. Stir in the parsley and seasoning to taste.

4 Drain the fish on absorbent kitchen paper and remove the cocktail sticks. Top the fishwith the golden crumbs, garnish with parsley sprigs and serve immediately with grilled tomato slices.

CHEESY FISH PIE WITH LEEKS

Serves: 4
Preparation time: 40 minutes
Cooking time: about 45 minutes
Freezing: suitable
675 cals per serving

700g (1½lb) floury potatoes

salt and freshly ground black pepper

450g (1lb) cod, haddock or whiting fillet

350ml (12fl oz) milk

350g (12oz) leeks

25g (1oz) butter

freshly grated nutmeg

225g (8oz) large prawns, cooked and peeled

SAUCE
50g (2oz) butter

45ml (3 tbsp) plain white flour

125g (4oz) blue Stilton cheese

60ml (4 tbsp) single cream

1 Peel the potatoes and cut into 5mm (¼ inch) thick slices. Bring a saucepan of salted water to the boil. Add the potatoes and cook for 5 minutes until partially softened. Drain.

2 Place the fish in a shallow pan. Pour on 50ml (2fl oz) of the milk. Season lightly, cover and poach for about 5 minutes until the fish flakes easily. Drain the fish, reserving the juices. Flake the fish, discarding the skin and any bones.

3 Trim and slice the leeks. Melt the butter in a pan and fry the leeks for 3 minutes, adding plenty of grated nutmeg. Lightly butter the sides of a 1.7 litre (3 pint) pie dish. Preheat the oven to 190°C/375°F/gas 5.

4 To make the sauce, melt the butter in a small saucepan. Add the flour and cook, stirring, for 1 minute. Remove from the heat and gradually blend in the milk and the reserved fish poaching juices.

5 Return to the heat and cook, stirring until thickened. Crumble in the cheese, then add the cream and seasoning.

6 Mix together the white fish, prawns and leeks in the prepared dish. Spoon over half of the cheese sauce. Layer the potatoes over the filling, then pour the remaining sauce over the potatoes. Place on a baking sheet and bake in the preheated oven for about 45 minutes until bubbling and turning golden. Serve hot, with a green vegetable.

TOP TIP
The pie can be frozen once assembled but before baking, provided the prawns used have not been previously frozen.

PARSLEY AND LEMON HADDOCK

Serves: 4
Preparation time: 10 minutes
Cooking time: 20–25 minutes
Freezing: not suitable
280 cals per serving

450g (1lb) fresh haddock fillet, skinned
45ml (3 tbsp) lemon juice
90ml (6 tbsp) chopped fresh parsley
salt and freshly ground black pepper
60ml (4 tbsp) water
50g (2oz) butter
45ml (3 tbsp) plain white flour
300ml (10fl oz) milk

1 Preheat the oven to 180°C/350°F/gas 4. Divide the fish into eight even-sized pieces and place in a shallow ovenproof dish. Sprinkle over the lemon juice with half the parsley and the seasoning. Add the water, then cover tightly.

2 Bake in the preheated oven for about 20–25 minutes, or until the fish flakes easily. Meanwhile, melt the butter in a pan then stir in the flour and cook for 1 minute. Gradually add the milk and bring to the boil. Reduce the heat and simmer for 2 minutes, stirring all the time.

3 Using a fish slice, lift the fish onto a serving platter, draining slightly, cover and keep warm. Add cooking juices to the sauce and reheat gently without boiling. Adjust the seasoning.

4 Spoon some of the sauce over the fish to serve, and garnish with the remaining parsley.

SMOKED HADDOCK DAUPHINOIS

Serves: 4
Preparation time: 15 minutes
Cooking time: about 1¼ hours
Freezing: suitable
535 cals per serving

450g (1lb) smoked haddock fillet

425ml (¾ pint) milk

1 leek

1 stick celery

15ml (1 tbsp) olive oil

salt and freshly ground black pepper

750g (1lb 10oz) floury potatoes

2 bay leaves

2 whole cloves

butter for greasing

150ml (¼ pint) crème fraîche

2.5ml (½ tsp) freshly ground nutmeg

25g (1oz) white breadcrumbs

1 Preheat the oven to 180°C/350°F/gas 4. Put the smoked haddock fillet into an ovenproof dish and pour over sufficient milk to cover the fish. Poach in the oven for 20 minutes, remove and put aside to cool. When the fish is cool enough to handle, drain the liquid into a jug and reserve. Flake the fish and leave on one side.

2 Wash and finely slice the leek and celery. Heat the olive oil in a pan and cook the sliced leek and celery until softened and all the water has evaporated. Season with salt and pepper and leave on one side.

3 Peel and slice the potatoes and gently cook in a large saucepan with any remaining milk, the bay leaves, cloves and the fish poaching liquid. The potatoes should be cooked but still a bit firm. Drain, reserving the cooking liquid.

4 When you are ready to assemble the dish, butter an ovenproof dish and spoon in the leeks and celery, and lay the flaked fish on top. Gently place the potato slices on top to cover the fish.

5 In a bowl, mix the crème fraîche with about 60ml (4 tbsp) of the reserved cooking milk. Season to taste with salt, pepper and nutmeg and spoon this mixture over the top of the potatoes.

6 Sprinkle the breadcrumbs over and bake in the oven for 30–40 minutes. Allow to stand for 5 minutes before serving.

CREAMY CASSEROLE OF SMOKED HADDOCK AND PRAWNS

Serves: 6
Preparation time: 20 minutes
Cooking time: 40 minutes
Freezing: not suitable
240 cals per serving

450g (1lb) fresh haddock fillet
225g (8oz) smoked haddock fillet
350g (12oz) onion, peeled
350g (12oz) old potatoes
175g (6oz) courgettes
175g (6oz) carrots, peeled
25g (1oz) butter or margarine
600ml (1 pint) light stock
125g (4oz) prawns, cooked and peeled
15ml (1 tbsp) cornflour
150ml (¼ pint) single cream
30–45ml (2–3 tbsp) chopped fresh parsley
freshly ground black pepper

1 Skin the haddock and cut the flesh into large pieces. Slice the onion. Peel the potatoes and cut into large chunks. Thickly slice the courgettes and carrots.

2 Melt the butter in a 4 litre (7 pint) flameproof casserole. Add the onion, courgettes and carrots and sauté gently, stirring, for 3–4 minutes.

3 Add the stock and potatoes and bring to the boil. Cover and simmer gently on the hob or cook in the oven at 170°C/325°F/gas 3 for 30 minutes or until all the vegetables are tender.

4 Add the haddock and prawns; bring back to the boil. Cover and simmer gently on the hob or return to the oven for a further 5 minutes until the fish is cooked.

5 Mix the cornflour to a smooth paste with a little water. Stir into the casserole and cook for 1 minute until slightly thickened, stirring all the time.

6 Just before serving, stir in the cream and parsley. Warm gently and season to taste with pepper. Serve in soup bowls, accompanied by crusty white bread.

KEDGEREE WITH HERB BUTTER

Serves: 4
Preparation time: 10 minutes
Cooking time: about 20 minutes
Freezing: not suitable
540 cals per serving

450g (1lb) smoked haddock

150ml (¼ pint) milk

75g (3oz) cooked cockles

5ml (1 tsp) coriander seeds

3 hard-boiled eggs

225g (8oz) basmati rice

30ml (2 tbsp) double cream

45–60ml (3–4 tbsp) chopped fresh chives

salt and freshly ground black pepper

lemon or lime wedges and extra herbs, to garnish

HERB BUTTER
50g (2oz) butter

5–10ml (1–2 tsp) lemon juice

30ml (2 tbsp) chopped fresh tarragon

1 Place the smoked haddock in a shallow pan with the milk. Cover and simmer gently for about 8 minutes until cooked through. Drain, reserving 30–45ml (2–3 tbsp) of the juices. Roughly flake the fish, discarding the skin and any bones.

2 Thoroughly drain the cockles. Finely crush the coriander seeds. Shell and quarter the eggs.

3 Cook the rice in plenty of boiling, salted water for 10 minutes or until just tender. Drain, rinse with boiling water and drain well.

4 Return the rice to the pan and add the flaked haddock, reserved cooking juices, cockles, coriander seeds, quartered eggs, cream and chives. Season lightly with salt and pepper and heat through gently for 2 minutes.

5 Meanwhile, for the herb butter, melt the butter and stir in the lemon juice, tarragon and a little seasoning. Pour into a warmed jug.

6 Spoon the kedgeree onto warmed serving plates and garnish with lemon or lime wedges and extra herbs. Serve accompanied by the herb butter.

TOP TIP
Choose natural undyed smoked haddock where possible. It's very pale by comparison to the familiar yellow smoked haddock because it doesn't contain colouring and it generally has a superior flavour.

VARIATIONS
• Use fresh salmon instead of smoked haddock.
• Replace the tarragon in the herb butter with dill or chervil.

MEAT AND POULTRY

ROAST LAMB WITH GARLIC AND MUSHROOM STUFFING

Serves: 8

Preparation time: 20 minutes, plus cooling

Cooking time: 2½–3 hours

Freezing: not suitable

560 cals per serving

225g (8oz) brown mushrooms

6 large garlic cloves

1 leek

60ml (4 tbsp) olive oil

45ml (3 tbsp) chopped fresh oregano

salt and freshly ground black pepper

2.3kg (5lb) boned leg of lamb

45–60ml (3–4 tbsp) redcurrant jelly

10ml (2 tsp) wine vinegar

150ml (¼ pint) red wine

300ml (½ pint) lamb stock

fresh herb sprigs, to garnish

1 Wipe the mushrooms and peel the garlic. Place both in a food processor and work briefly until finely chopped. Trim and chop the leek. Heat the oil in a frying pan. Add the mushrooms, garlic and leek and fry for about 10 minutes until the mushroom juices have evaporated and the mixture has the consistency of a thick paste. Stir in the oregano and season with salt and pepper. Leave to cool.

2 Preheat the oven to 180°C/350°F/gas 4. Open out the lamb and pack the stuffing down the centre. Fold the meat over the stuffing to enclose and tie with string. Place the lamb, joined-side down, in a roasting tin.

3 Roast the lamb in the preheated oven for 25 minutes per 450g (1lb) of meat plus 25 minutes for medium done; or for 30 minutes per 450g (1lb) of meat plus 30 minutes for well done.

4 Melt the redcurrant jelly in a small saucepan with the wine vinegar. Thirty minutes before the end of the roasting time, brush the lamb with the redcurrant glaze. Repeat several times before the end of the cooking time.

5 Remove the lamb from the tin and transfer to a warmed serving platter. Keep warm. Drain off the fat from the pan and stir in the wine and stock. Bring to the boil and boil until slightly reduced. Strain the gravy, if preferred, into a warmed sauceboat.

6 Remove the string from the lamb. Surround with herbs and serve accompanied by the gravy and vegetables of your choice.

VARIATION
Whole roasted garlic bulbs make an attractive and delicious garnish. Roast them in their skins around the meat in the roasting tin.

SPICY LAMB CHUMP CHOPS WITH PEPPERS AND BUTTERNUT SQUASH

Serves: 4
Preparation time: 20 minutes
Cooking time: 30 minutes
Freezing: suitable
655 cals per serving

4 lean lamb chump chops, each weighing about 150–175g (5–6oz)

1 onion, peeled

2 garlic cloves, peeled

1 red pepper, halved and deseeded

1 yellow pepper, halved and deseeded

30ml (2 tbsp) olive oil

1 small butternut squash, weighing about 700g (1lb 9oz)

4 whole cloves

1 x 5cm (2 inch) piece cinnamon stick

1 x 400g (14oz) can chopped tomatoes

15ml (1 tbsp) of tomato purée

salt and pepper

15ml (1 tbsp) chopped fresh coriander

MARINADE
5ml (1 tsp) coriander seeds

5ml (1 tsp) cumin seeds

juice of ½ lemon

30ml (2 tbsp) extra-virgin olive oil

salt and freshly ground black pepper

2 garlic cloves, peeled and chopped

1 First prepare the marinade. Toast the coriander and cumin seeds by shaking them over a low heat in a dry pan until brown and fragrant, then grind in a pestle and mortar or electric spice grinder (a clean coffee grinder will do the job). Mix in a bowl the ground spices with the lemon juice, olive oil, salt and pepper to taste and chopped garlic.

2 Smear the marinade over the chump chops and put aside for 30 minutes.

3 Chop the onion, crush the garlic and cut the peppers into large dice.

4 Heat the olive oil in a large saucepan and add the prepared onion, garlic and peppers. Leave to cook gently.

5 Meanwhile peel and cut the butternut squash into cubes and add to the saucepan along with the cloves and cinnamon stick and cook for 5 minutes.

6 Pour in the can of tomatoes, add the tomato purée and season to taste. Cover and cook for 20 minutes or until the squash is soft, then stir in the chopped coriander. Keep warm while you cook the lamb.

7 Preheat the grill to high, and cook the chump chops for about 4 minutes on each side, or longer according to taste and the thickness of the chops. Serve immediately with the hot vegetables.

LAMB 'TOAD-IN-THE-HOLE' WITH CREAMY ONION SAUCE

Serves: 4
Preparation time: 25 minutes
Cooking time: about 40 minutes
Freezing: not suitable
510 cals per serving

8 lamb cutlets

2 cloves garlic, peeled and crushed

15ml (1 tbsp) oil

flat-leaf parsley and thyme sprigs, to garnish

BATTER
125g (4oz) plain flour

pinch of salt

2 eggs

300ml (½ pint) milk

15ml (1 tbsp) chopped fresh parsley

15ml (1 tbsp) chopped fresh rosemary or thyme

SAUCE
1 large onion

25g (1oz) butter

15ml (1 tbsp) plain flour

300ml (½ pint) milk

2.5ml (½ tsp) ground mace

1 bay leaf

30ml (2 tbsp) double cream

salt and freshly ground black pepper

1 Preheat the oven to 220°C/425°F/gas 7. Trim excess fat from the lamb cutlets, then spread with the garlic. Heat the oil in a frying pan and fry the lamb on both sides until sealed and browned.

2 Lightly grease the sides of a shallow 1.2 litre (2 pint) ovenproof dish. Lay the lamb cutlets in the dish, propping the thin ends up to raise them slightly.

3 To make the batter, sift the flour and salt into a bowl. Make a well in the centre and add the eggs with a little of the milk. Whisk together the eggs and remaining milk, gradually incorporating the flour to make a paste. Beat in the remaining milk and herbs.

4 Cook the lamb in the preheated oven for 5 minutes, then pour the batter around the lamb and return to the oven. Reduce the temperature to 200°C/400°F/gas 6 and cook for a further 35 minutes or until the batter is well risen and crisp.

5 Meanwhile make the sauce. Peel and finely chop the onion. Melt the butter in a saucepan and fry the onion for about 3 minutes, until beginning to colour. Stir in the flour, then gradually blend in the milk. Add the mace and bay leaf and cook, stirring, for 1 minute until slightly thickened. Leave to simmer very gently for 10 minutes until thickened. Remove the bay leaf and add the cream and seasoning.

6 Serve the lamb in batter piping hot, garnished with herbs and accompanied by the onion sauce.

TOP TIP
If you prefer lamb slightly pink, choose thick cutlets and omit the 5 minutes pre-baking. Instead, simply preheat the dish, with a little oil added.

VARIATIONS
- *Use 450g (1lb) good-quality sausages instead of the lamb.*
- *Replace the lamb with chunks of rump steak and kidney.*

IRISH STEW

Serves: 4
Preparation time: 15 minutes
Cooking time: 2 hours
Freezing: suitable
490 cals per serving

700g (1½lb) middle neck lamb cutlets

2 onions, peeled

450g (1lb) old potatoes, peeled

15ml (1 tbsp) chopped fresh parsley

5ml (1 tsp) dried thyme

salt and freshly ground black pepper

300ml (½ pint) lamb stock or water

chopped fresh parsley, to garnish

1 Preheat the oven to 170°C/325°F/gas 3. Trim excess fat from the meat. Thinly slice the onions and potatoes.

2 Layer the meat, onions and potatoes in a deep casserole, sprinkling each layer with the herbs and seasoning.

3 Finish with an overlapping layer of potato. Pour in the stock or water. Cover with greaseproof paper, then the lid.

4 Cook in the hot oven for about 2 hours or until the meat and vegetables are tender. Uncover and place under a hot grill to brown the top, if desired. Sprinkle with parsley to serve.

SAUSAGES 'N' BEANS

Serves: 4
Preparation time: 15 minutes
Cooking time: 35 minutes
Freezing: suitable
1055 cals per serving

2 x 400g (14oz) packs good-quality pork sausages

15ml (1 tbsp) olive oil

1 onion, peeled and finely chopped

15ml (1 tbsp) red wine

15ml (1 tbsp) tomato purée

1 x 250g (9oz) can chopped tomatoes

2 x 400g (14oz) cans flageolet beans

15ml (1tbsp) roughly chopped fresh flat-leaf parsley

few sprigs of fresh rosemary, washed and leaves removed from the stalks and chopped

salt and freshly ground black pepper

5ml (1 tsp) sugar

1 Preheat the oven to 200°C/400°F/gas 6. Place the sausages in a lightly greased roasting tin and prick their skins. Bake in the hot oven for 30 minutes or until cooked through and browned.

2 Meanwhile, heat the oil in a saucepan and add the finely chopped onion. Slowly cook until the onion is softened and browned. Stir in the red wine, scraping any residue off the bottom of the pan, then add the tomato purée and the chopped tomatoes. Stir and cook for 15 minutes until the sauce has reduced and has become syrupy.

3 Drain and rinse the flageolet beans and add to the tomato sauce with the chopped parsley and rosemary, seasoning and a sprinkling of sugar to taste. Heat through for 5 minutes so the flavours are absorbed.

4 As soon as the sausages are ready, serve with the hot beans.

PORK WITH PRUNES

Serves: 4

Preparation time: 10 minutes, plus marinating

Cooking time: 40 minutes

Freezing: not suitable

600 cals per serving

12 large prunes, pitted

300ml (½ pint) fruity, dry white wine

8 thin pork chops or steaks, weighing about 1.4kg (3lb) in total

salt and freshly ground black pepper

flour, for coating

25g (1oz) butter

300ml (½ pint) light stock

10ml (2 tsp) redcurrant jelly

thyme sprigs, to garnish

1 Put the prunes and wine in a bowl, cover and soak overnight.

2 Dip the pork chops in seasoned flour to coat. Melt the butter in a flameproof casserole and brown the chops in two batches. Return all the chops to the pan. Pour in the stock, wine and prunes. Bring to the boil, cover and simmer gently for about 30 minutes or until the pork is tender, turning the meat once. Transfer the pork and prunes to a warmed platter, cover and keep warm.

3 Whisk the redcurrant jelly into the cooking liquid. Bring to the boil and boil for about 4–5 minutes until the sauce has reduced slightly. Taste and adjust the seasoning, then pour the sauce over the meat. Garnish with thyme and serve immediately.

PORK AND APPLE STROGANOFF

Serves: 4
Preparation time: 10 minutes
Cooking time: 15 minutes
Freezing: suitable
360 cals per serving

450g (1lb) lean pork tenderloin or fillet

15ml (1 tbsp) olive oil

10g (¼oz) butter

2 eating apples

1 onion

2 garlic cloves

30ml (2 tbsp) Calvados or brandy

150ml (¼ pint) crème fraîche

salt and freshly ground black pepper

1 Slice the pork tenderloin or fillet across the grain of the meat to produce thin rounds about 8mm (⅜ inch) thick. Season well.

2 Warm the oil and melt the butter in a large heavy-based frying pan. Brown the pork and put aside. Core and slice the apples into wedges, add to the pan and cook until slightly softened and coloured. Remove and put aside with the pork.

3 Peel and slice the onion. Peel and chop the garlic. Fry the onion and garlic in the frying pan until softened and browning at the edges. Add the Calvados or brandy to the pan and stir to dislodge any residue that has stuck to the bottom of the pan.

4 Add the crème fraîche and return the pork and apples to the pan. Season and bring to the boil, then lower the heat and simmer for 5 minutes – the apples should be soft but not falling apart. Serve immediately with boiled rice.

BOILED BACON WITH PARSLEY SAUCE

Serves: 6–8
Preparation time: 10 minutes
Cooking time: 1¼–1½ hours
Freezing: not suitable
515–385 cals per serving

1.4kg (3lb) gammon, collar or forehock bacon joint

2 onions, peeled and quartered

2 carrots, peeled and quartered

2 celery sticks, chopped

1 bay leaf

4 black peppercorns

fresh parsley sprigs, to garnish

PARSLEY SAUCE
300ml (½ pint) milk

1 slice of onion

1 bay leaf

6 peppercorns

15g (½oz) butter

15g (½oz) plain flour

salt and freshly ground black pepper

30ml (2 tbsp) chopped fresh parsley

1 Weigh the joint and calculate the cooking time, allowing 20 minutes per 450g (1lb) plus 20 minutes.

2 To remove the salt, place the joint in a large saucepan with enough cold water to cover. Slowly bring to the boil, then discard the water.

3 Place the joint in a large saucepan with the vegetables, bay leaf and peppercorns. Cover with cold water and bring slowly to the boil. Skim the surface with a slotted spoon. Cover and simmer gently for the calculated cooking time.

4 Meanwhile make the sauce. Pour the milk into a saucepan. Add the slice of onion, bay leaf and peppercorns. Bring to almost boiling, remove from the heat, cover and leave to stand for 10–30 minutes. Strain.

5 Melt the butter in a saucepan. Stir in the flour and cook, stirring, for 1 minute. Remove from the heat and gradually pour on the warm milk, whisking constantly. Season lightly with salt and pepper, then stir in the chopped parsley.

6 When the bacon is cooked, ease off the rind and remove any excess fat. Carve into slices and serve hot, garnished with parsley and accompanied by the parsley sauce.

STEAK AND KIDNEY PUDDING

Serves: 6
Preparation time: 35 minutes
Cooking time: about 3½ hours
Freezing: not suitable
540 cals per serving

FILLING
700g (1½lb) braising or stewing steak

225g (8oz) ox kidney

60ml (4 tbsp) plain flour

salt and freshly ground black pepper

2 small onions

45ml (3 tbsp) oil

450ml (¾ pint) beef stock

90ml (6 tbsp) port

225g (8oz) mushrooms

8 canned smoked oysters (optional)

PASTRY
300g (10oz) self-raising flour

2.5ml (½ tsp) salt

150g (5oz) suet

1 Trim the meat and cut into 2cm (¾ inch) pieces. Remove the white core from the kidney, then cut into 1cm (½ inch) chunks. Season the flour with salt and pepper and use to coat the meat.

2 Peel and chop the onions. Heat the oil in a large frying pan and fry the steak in batches until browned on all sides. Transfer to a flameproof casserole or heavy-based saucepan, using a slotted spoon. Brown the kidney in the oil remaining in the frying pan, then transfer to the casserole. Add the onion to the frying pan and fry gently for about 10 minutes until soft, adding a little extra oil if necessary. Add to the meat with the stock, port and seasoning. Bring to the boil, reduce the heat, cover and simmer gently for 1¼ hours.

3 To make the pastry, sift the flour and salt into a bowl and stir in the suet. Add 175ml (6fl oz) cold water and mix to a soft dough using a round-bladed knife, adding a little extra water if the pastry is dry.

4 Roll out a scant three quarters of the dough on a lightly floured surface. Use to line a 1.7 litre (3 pint) pudding basin.

5 Halve any large mushrooms and stir the mushrooms into the meat with the oysters if using. Turn into the lined basin. Brush the top edge of the pastry with water. Roll out the remainder to make a lid and lay over the pudding, pressing the edges together to seal.

6 Cover the basin with a pleated, double thickness layer of greaseproof paper, securing under the rim with string. Cover with foil and place in a steamer or on an upturned saucer in a large saucepan. Pour in enough hot water to come halfway up the sides of the basin. Cover with a lid and steam for 2 hours, checking the water level occasionally.

7 Remove the foil and greaseproof paper and loosen the edges of the pudding. Invert onto a serving plate and serve at once, with vegetables in season.

PEPPERED STEAK

Serves: 4
Preparation time: 10 minutes
Cooking time: 6–12 minutes
Freezing: not suitable
515 cals per serving

4 sirloin, rump or fillet steaks

30ml (2 tbsp) black or green peppercorns, coarsely crushed

25g (1oz) butter or margarine

15ml (1 tbsp) oil

salt

30ml (2 tbsp) brandy

150ml (¼ pint) double cream

1 Trim excess fat from the steaks, then place on the crushed peppercorns and press hard to encrust the surface of the meat. Turn to encrust the other side.

2 Heat the butter and oil in a frying pan and fry the steaks for 2 minutes on each side. Reduce the heat and continue cooking until cooked to taste. Season with salt.

3 Remove the steaks from the pan and keep warm. Add the brandy to the pan, remove from the heat and set it alight.

4 When the flames have died down, stir in the cream; reheat gently. Pour over the steaks and serve immediately.

TRADITIONAL ROAST BEEF AND YORKSHIRE PUDDING

Serves: 6–8
Preparation time: 20 minutes
Cooking time: variable (depends on size of joint)
Freezing: not suitable
755 cals per serving

1.4–1.8kg (3–4lb) sirloin, rib, rump or topside

25g (1oz) beef dripping (optional)

salt and freshly ground black pepper

5ml (1 tsp) mustard powder (optional)

YORKSHIRE PUDDING
125g (4oz) plain flour

pinch of salt

1 egg

300ml (½ pint) milk

GRAVY
10ml (2 tsp) plain flour

300ml (½ pint) beef stock

1 Preheat the oven to 180°C/350°F/gas 4. Place the meat in a shallow roasting tin, preferably on a roasting rack, with the thickest layer of fat uppermost and the cut sides exposed to the heat. Add dripping if the meat is lean. Season the meat with pepper and mustard powder, if wished.

2 Roast the beef in the preheated oven for 20 minutes per 450g (1lb) of meat plus 20 minutes for rare; or 25 minutes per 450g (1lb) of meat plus 25 minutes for medium done; or 30 minutes per 450g (1lb) of meat plus 30 minutes for well done. Baste occasionally with the juices from the tin. Forty-five minutes before the end of the cooking time, cover the joint with foil and place on the bottom shelf of the oven, then increase the oven temperature to 220°C/425°F/gas 7.

3 To make the Yorkshire pudding, mix the flour and salt in a bowl, then make a well in the centre and break in the egg. Add half the milk and, using a wooden spoon, gradually work in the flour. Beat the mixture until it is smooth, then add the remaining milk and 100ml (3½fl oz) water. Beat until well mixed and the surface is covered with tiny bubbles.

4 Put 30ml (2 tbsp) fat from the beef into a baking tin and place in the oven at 220°C/425°F/gas 7 for a few minutes until the fat is very hot.

5 Pour in the batter and return to the oven to cook for 40–45 minutes, until risen and golden brown; do not open the oven door for 30 minutes.

6 After 30 minutes, transfer the cooked meat to a warmed serving plate and leave to rest for about 20 minutes, covered, before carving.

7 To make the gravy, the meat juices alone may be used. For a thicker gravy, skim some of the fat from the surface and place the tin over moderate heat. Sprinkle the flour into the tin and stir it into the pan juices, scraping up the brown sediment. Cook over high heat, stirring constantly, until the flour has browned slightly. (When the meat is carved, any juices from the meat can be added to the gravy.) Add up to 300ml (½ pint) beef stock to the tin and stir well. Bring it to the boil, simmer for 2–3 minutes and season to taste. Pour into a sauceboat or jug.

8 Serve the carved beef with Yorkshire pudding, cut into portions. Accompany with the gravy and mustard or horseradish sauce, and seasonal vegetables.

BEEF AND BEER STEW WITH PARSNIP PURÉE

Serves: 6
Preparation time: 25 minutes
Cooking time: about 1¾ hours
Freezing: suitable (for beef and beer stew only)
500 cals per serving

1.1kg (2½lb) chuck or blade beef
30ml (2 tbsp) plain flour
salt and freshly ground black pepper
3 large onions
4 celery sticks
several fresh thyme sprigs
2 bay leaves
450g (1lb) turnips
25g (1oz) beef dripping or lard
450ml (¾ pint) beef stock
450ml (¾ pint) strong beer
45ml (3 tbsp) black treacle
celery leaves, to garnish

PARSNIP PURÉE
900g (2lb) parsnips
45ml (3 tbsp) double cream

1 Cut the meat into large chunks, discarding excess fat. Season the flour with salt and pepper and use to coat the meat. Peel and thinly slice the onions. Cut two 5cm (2 inch) lengths of celery. Tie in bundles with the thyme and bay leaves. Cut the remaining celery into chunks. Peel the turnips and cut into large chunks.

2 Preheat the oven to 160°C/325°F/gas 3. Heat the dripping or lard in a large flameproof casserole. Add half of the meat and fry, turning, until lightly browned. Remove with a slotted spoon and fry the remainder; remove from the pan.

3 Add the onions and celery to the pan and fry gently until softened. Return the meat to the pan and add the herb bundles. Stir in the stock, beer and treacle, then add the turnips. Bring just to the boil, reduce the heat, cover with a lid and transfer to the oven. Cook for 1½ hours or until the meat and vegetables are tender.

4 Peel the parsnips and cut into 7.5cm (3 inch) lengths; cut lengthwise into even-sized pieces. Put the parsnips into a saucepan and cover with water. Bring to the boil, lower the heat and simmer for about 15 minutes until completely tender.

5 Drain the parsnips thoroughly and return to the pan. Add the cream and seasoning and mash well until completely smooth.

6 Divide the stew between warmed serving plates and add spoonfuls of the parsnip purée. Garnish with celery leaves.

VARIATION
Use Guinness instead of beer.

SCOTCH BEEF COLLOPS

Serves: 4
Preparation time: 10 minutes
Cooking time: 15–20 minutes
Freezing: not suitable
390 cals per serving

8 steaks, each weighing about 75g (3oz)

flour, for coating

salt and freshly ground black pepper

50g (2oz) unsalted butter

grated rind of ½ lemon

pinch of ground mace

150ml (¼ pint) white wine

1 egg yolk

45ml (3 tbsp) double cream

roughly chopped fresh parsley, to garnish

1 Trim the steaks if necessary and, using a rolling pin, beat out thinly between two sheets of greaseproof paper. Lightly dust the steaks with seasoned flour.

2 Melt the butter in a large frying pan and, when foaming, brown the steaks well on both sides in two batches.

3 Return all the steaks to the pan and add the lemon rind, mace and wine. Bring to the boil, then simmer uncovered for about 5 minutes until tender. Transfer the meat to a serving dish; keep warm.

4 Boil the sauce to reduce slightly. Beat the egg yolk and cream together in a bowl, then stir into the sauce and heat through, without boiling, until slightly thickened; season with salt and pepper to taste. Strain.

5 Garnish the meat with parsley and serve with the sauce, new potatoes and a green vegetable.

ROAST CHICKEN WITH DEVILLED SAUCE

Serves: 6
Preparation time: 20 minutes
Cooking time: about 1¾ hours
Freezing: not suitable
270 cals per serving

3 garlic cloves

1 large onion

2.3kg (5lb) large chicken

90ml (3fl oz) crème fraîche

fresh leafy herbs, such as basil or lemon balm, to garnish

DEVILLED SAUCE
30ml (2 tbsp) mango or sweet fruit chutney

25g (1oz) butter

30ml (2 tbsp) Worcestershire sauce

30ml (2 tbsp) grainy English mustard

5ml (1 tsp) paprika

45ml (3 tbsp) freshly squeezed orange juice

salt and freshly ground black pepper

450g (1lb) tomatoes

1 Preheat the oven to 190°C/375°F/gas 5. To make the devilled sauce, chop any large pieces in the chutney. Melt the butter. Mix together the butter, chutney, Worcestershire sauce, mustard, paprika, orange juice and seasoning.

2 Peel and chop the garlic and onion; place in the cavity of the chicken, then place the chicken in a roasting tin. Baste the skin all over with the devilled sauce. Roast in the oven, basting frequently with the sauce for 1¾ hours, or until the juices run clear when the thickest part of the thigh is pierced with a skewer. At the end of the cooking time the chicken should be slightly charred, but cover with foil towards the end of cooking if it becomes over-blackened.

3 In the meantime, place the tomatoes in a bowl and cover with boiling water. Leave for 1 minute, then drain and peel away the skins. Scoop out the seeds, then roughly chop the tomatoes; set aside.

4 Transfer the chicken to a warmed serving platter and keep warm. Skim off the fat from the juices in the roasting tin, then stir in the tomatoes and any remaining devilled sauce. Transfer the sauce to a food processor or blender and process briefly until the mixture is pulpy but retaining a little texture. Return to the pan and heat through, seasoning with salt and pepper to taste.

5 Meanwhile warm the crème fraîche in a small saucepan.

6 Garnish the chicken with plenty of herbs and serve with the devilled sauce and crème fraîche.

VARIATION
For a more fiery sauce, add a finely chopped chilli to the devilled mixture before basting.

HERBY CHICKEN BREASTS

Serves: 4
Preparation time: 10 minutes
Cooking time: 20 minutes
Freezing: suitable
330 cals per serving

75g (3oz) unsalted butter, softened

15ml (1 tbsp) chopped chives

15ml (1tbsp) chopped fresh tarragon

15ml (1 tbsp) chopped fresh flat-leaf parsley

finely grated rind and juice of 1 lemon

2 garlic cloves, peeled and finely chopped

salt

4 chicken breasts, skinless, each weighing about 175g (6oz)

1 Preheat the oven to 180°C/350°F/gas 4. Place the butter in a small bowl and mash in the chopped herbs, then the lemon rind, chopped garlic and a pinch of salt to make a thick paste.

2 Make 4 or 5 slashes across each chicken breast and place the breasts in an oven dish. With your fingers rub the butter paste onto the chicken pieces, making sure it is worked well into the slashes.

3 Place the chicken in the preheated oven and cook for 20 minutes, basting periodically. To check the chicken is cooked, press a small knife or skewer through the flesh; the juices should run clear with no signs of blood.

4 Pour the lemon juice over the chicken and serve immediately.

CHICKEN AND HAM PIE

Serves: 4–6
Preparation time: 20 minutes
Cooking time: 30 minutes
Freezing: not suitable
860–570 cals per serving

700g (1½lb) cooked chicken or turkey

225g (8oz) cooked gammon or ham

2 leeks

350g (12oz) mascarpone or other cream cheese

1 egg

5ml (1 tsp) mustard

45ml (3 tbsp) chopped fresh parsley

5ml (1 tsp) finely grated lemon rind

225g (8oz) ready-made flaky or puff pastry

salt and freshly ground black pepper

beaten egg, to glaze

1 Preheat the oven to 200°C/400°F/gas 6. Cut the chicken or turkey and the gammon or ham into large chunks. Trim the leeks and cut into 2.5cm (1 inch) slices. Bring a small saucepan of water to the boil. Add the leeks, bring to the boil again and cook for about 2 minutes or until slightly softened. Drain thoroughly, reserving 45ml (3 tbsp) of the cooking liquid.

2 Put the mascarpone in a bowl and mix with the reserved cooking liquid. Gradually beat in the egg, then add the mustard, parsley, lemon rind and plenty of salt and pepper. Fold in the chicken or turkey, with the gammon or ham and the leeks. Spoon the mixture into a 1.4 litre (2½ pint) pie dish. If you have a pie funnel, push it down into the middle of the filling to support the pastry.

3 Roll out the pastry on a lightly floured surface and trim to an oval about 5cm (2 inches) larger than the pie dish. Cut off a 2.5cm (1 inch) strip from all round the oval and press onto the rim of the pie dish.

4 Brush the pastry rim with a little beaten egg, then position the pastry oval on top to make a lid. Press the edges together to seal then, using a sharp knife, knock up the edges. Make a slit in the middle to let steam escape, allowing the funnel to show through if using.

5 Decorate with leaves cut from the pastry trimmings, if desired. Brush the pastry thoroughly with beaten egg.

6 Stand the pie on a baking sheet. Bake in the preheated oven for about 30 minutes or until the pastry is well risen and dark golden brown. Leave to cool and settle for 15 minutes before cutting.

CHICKEN WITH TARRAGON

Serves: 4

Preparation time: 20 minutes

Cooking time: 20–25 minutes

Freezing: not suitable

335 cals per serving

4 skinless chicken breast fillets, each weighing about 150g (5oz)

salt and freshly ground black pepper

flour, for coating

25g (1oz) butter

75ml (5 tbsp) dry white wine

60ml (4 tbsp) chicken stock

6 juniper berries, lightly crushed

150ml (¼ pint) single cream

15ml (1 tbsp) chopped fresh tarragon

1 Dip the chicken breasts in seasoned flour to coat evenly, shaking off any excess.

2 Heat the butter in a sauté pan and brown the chicken breasts on both sides. Add the wine, stock and juniper berries. Cook, covered, over a low heat for 10–12 minutes.

3 Add the cream, seasoning and tarragon. Cook gently for a further 5–10 minutes, or until the thicken is cooked through; do not allow to boil.

CHICKEN BREASTS STUFFED WITH MUSHROOMS

Serves: 6
Preparation time: 25 minutes
Cooking time: 25–30 minutes
Freezing: suitable (for herb butter only)
500 cals per serving

1 shallot
30ml (2 tbsp) olive oil
125g (4oz) small open cup mushrooms
40g (1½oz) mild creamy goat's cheese
2 thin slices of Parma ham
45ml (3 tbsp) chopped fresh parsley
salt and freshly ground black pepper
125g (4oz) butter
30ml (2 tbsp) chopped fresh basil
squeeze of lemon juice
6 chicken breast fillets, with skin

1 Peel and very finely chop the shallot. Heat the oil in a heavy-based frying pan, add the shallot and cook gently until softened but not browned. Meanwhile, finely chop the mushrooms. When the shallots are softened, add the mushrooms to the pan and continue cooking until they are well reduced and softened.

2 Remove the pan from the heat, allow to cool slightly, then add the goat's cheese. Finely chop the Parma ham and add to the mixture with half of the parsley and plenty of salt and pepper. Leave the stuffing to cool completely. Preheat the oven to 200°C/400°F/gas 6.

3 Meanwhile, make the herb butter. Beat 75g (3oz) of the butter until soft, then add the remaining parsley, the basil, lemon juice and salt and pepper. Dollop the butter onto a sheet of greaseproof paper and shape into a small sausage using the paper to help you roll it into a neat even shape. Chill in the refrigerator until firm.

4 When the stuffing is cold, carefully loosen the skin from each chicken breast, making sure you keep it attached along one long side.

5 Carefully spoon the stuffing under the chicken skin. Tie the chicken into a neat parcel with string, or secure the filling by pushing a fine wooden skewer through the skin. Lay the chicken in a roasting tin, stuffed-side uppermost.

6 Melt the remaining butter and brush over the chicken. Season with salt and pepper. Roast in the preheated oven for 25–30 minutes or until cooked right through.

7 Cut the herb butter into thin slices. Transfer the chicken breasts to warmed serving plates and top with a couple of slices of herb butter. Serve immediately.

HEARTY CHICKEN AND VEGETABLE STEW

Serves: 4–6
Preparation time: 15–20 minutes
Cooking time: about 1 hour
Freezing: suitable
580–390 cals per serving

1 chicken, about 1.4kg (3lb) or 4 chicken quarters

30ml (2 tbsp) white flour

salt and freshly ground black pepper

30ml (2 tbsp) olive oil

2 onions

2 parsnips

2 large carrots

2 large potatoes

125g (4oz) split red lentils

2 bay leaves

2 garlic cloves (optional)

425g (15oz) can black-eye or red kidney beans, drained

2 courgettes, sliced

45ml (3 tbsp) chopped fresh parsley

15ml (1 tbsp) snipped fresh chives (optional)

1 Joint the chicken; if using chicken quarters, cut each in half. Sprinkle the chicken with flour and season with salt and pepper.

2 Heat the oil in a flameproof casserole and cook the chicken in batches until well browned on all sides. Remove from the casserole and set aside.

3 Meanwhile, peel the onions and chop roughly. Peel the parsnips, carrots and potatoes; cut them all into chunks. Add a little extra oil to the casserole if necessary and cook the vegetables until lightly browned.

4 Return the chicken to the casserole and add the lentils, bay leaves, garlic if using, and 900ml (1½ pints) water. Cover with a tight-fitting lid and simmer gently, stirring occasionally, for 45 minutes or until the chicken is tender and the lentils are soft and mushy.

5 Rinse the kidney beans, drain and add to the casserole with the courgettes. Season to taste with salt and pepper. Cook for a further 15 minutes or until the courgettes are just tender and the beans are heated through. If the sauce is too thin, retrieve a few spoonfuls of vegetables, mash them with a potato masher and return to the stew to thicken it slightly. Sprinkle with the chopped parsley, and chives if using. Serve immediately.

TOP TIP
Before using canned beans, always tip them into a sieve and rinse thoroughly under cold running water to remove the slimy residue.

COQ AU VIN

Serves: 8
Preparation time: 30 minutes
Cooking time: 1¼–1½ hours
Freezing: not suitable
510 cals per serving

1 large chicken jointed, or
8 chicken joints

30ml (2 tbsp) plain flour

salt and freshly ground black
pepper

125g (4oz) butter

125g (4oz) lean bacon, diced

1 onion peeled and quartered

1 carrot, quartered

60ml (4 tbsp) brandy

600ml (1 pint) red wine

1 garlic clove, peeled and crushed

1 bouquet garni

1 sugar lump

30ml (2 tbsp) oil

450g (1lb) button onions, peeled

pinch of sugar

5ml (1 tsp) wine vinegar

225g (8oz) button mushrooms

6 slices of white bread, crusts
removed

1 Coat the chicken pieces with 15ml (1 tbsp) of the flour, liberally seasoned with salt and pepper. Melt 25g (1oz) of the butter in a flameproof casserole, add the chicken pieces and fry gently until they are golden brown on all sides. Add the bacon, onion and carrot and fry until softened.

2 Heat the brandy in a small saucepan, pour over the chicken and ignite, shaking the pan so that all the chicken pieces are covered in flames. Pour on the wine and stir to loosen any sediment from the bottom of the casserole. Add the garlic, bouquet garni and sugar lump. Bring to the boil, cover and simmer gently for 1–1¼ hours or until tender.

3 Meanwhile, melt another 25g (1oz) of the butter with 10ml (2 tsp) of the oil in a frying pan. Add the button onions and fry until they begin to brown. Add the sugar and vinegar, together with 15ml (1 tbsp) water. Cover and cook for 10–15 minutes or until just tender. Keep warm.

4 Melt 25g (1oz) butter with 10ml (2 tsp) oil in a frying pan and sauté the mushrooms for a few minutes until tender; keep warm. Remove the chicken and vegetables from the casserole, place in a serving dish with the onions and mushrooms and keep hot. Discard the bouquet garni. Skim off excess fat, then, boil the liquid briskly for 3–5 minutes to reduce it.

5 Heat the remaining oil in a frying pan and fry the bread until crisp and golden brown on both sides. Cut into triangles.

6 Work the remaining flour and butter together to make a beurre manié. Off the heat, whisk into the cooking liquid in small pieces. Cook, stirring, until the sauce is thick and shiny. Adjust the seasoning and pour over the chicken. Garnish with the fried bread.

TRADITIONAL ROAST DUCK

Serves: 4–6

Preparation time: 25 minutes

Cooking time: depends on size

Freezing: not suitable

330 cals per serving

1 oven-ready duckling

salt and freshly ground black pepper

1 onion, peeled

25g (1oz) butter

1 small eating apple

100g (4oz) fresh wholemeal breadcrumbs

15ml (1 tbsp) chopped sage or 5ml (1 tsp) dried sage

1 egg

450g (1lb) cooking apples

a little sugar (optional)

1 Preheat the oven to 180°C/350°F/gas 4. Weigh the duckling to calculate the cooking time. Prick the skin all over with a skewer or sharp fork and sprinkle with salt. (This helps to draw out the fat and crisp the skin.)

2 To make the stuffing, finely chop the onion. Melt half the butter in a saucepan and cook the onion gently until softened but not browned. Peel, core and grate the eating apple and stir into the onion with the breadcrumbs, sage, egg and seasoning. Shape the stuffing into small balls and place in a roasting tin.

3 Place the duckling on a wire rack or trivet in a roasting tin. Roast in the preheated oven for 30–35 minutes per 450g (1lb) of meat. Cook the stuffing balls for the last 30 minutes of the calculated time.

4 Meanwhile, make the apple sauce. Peel, core and slice the apples. Place in a heavy-based saucepan with 15ml (1 tbsp) water. Cover tightly and cook for about 10 minutes, until the apples are tender, shaking the pan occasionally. Stir in the remaining butter and beat with a wooden spoon until smooth. Stir in a little sugar, if liked. Carve the duckling and serve with the apple sauce and thin gravy.

TOP TIP

Make sure you buy a large enough duckling – there is much less flesh on a duck than on a chicken of the same weight. Allow at least 450g (1lb) dressed weight per person.

PUDDINGS AND DESSERTS

SPICED RAISIN PUDDINGS WITH DEMERARA LEMON BUTTER

Serves: 8
Preparation time: 25 minutes
Cooking time: 40–45 minutes
Freezing: suitable (see Top Tip)
560 cals per serving

1 piece preserved stem ginger in syrup, weighing about 15g (½oz)

175g (6oz) unsalted butter, softened

175g (6oz) caster sugar

3 eggs, lightly beaten

225g (8oz) self-raising flour

7.5ml (1½ tsp) baking powder

5ml (1 tsp) ground mixed spice

2.5ml (½ tsp) ground cinnamon

75g (3oz) raisins

a little milk

cream or crème fraîche, to serve

SAUCE
75g (3oz) unsalted butter

175g (6oz) demerara sugar

grated rind and juice of 2 small lemons

1 Preheat the oven to 180°C/350°F/gas 4. Grease the bases and sides of eight individual 185ml (6fl oz) metal pudding basins. Chop the ginger into tiny pieces.

2 In a bowl, cream together the butter and sugar until pale and fluffy. Add the eggs, a little at a time, beating well after each addition, and adding a little of the flour to prevent curdling.

3 Sift the remaining flour, baking powder and spices over the bowl. Add the raisins and chopped ginger and gradually fold in, using a large metal spoon. Stir in sufficient milk to give a soft, dropping consistency.

4 Divide the mixture among the prepared tins and level the surfaces. Stand in a roasting tin and pour boiling water around the tins to a depth of 1cm (½ inch). Cover the roasting tin with foil. Bake in the preheated oven for 40–45 minutes until the sponges have risen and feel firm to the touch.

5 Meanwhile, make the sauce. Melt the butter in a small saucepan. Add the sugar and heat gently for 2–3 minutes until bubbling. Add the lemon rind and juice and cook gently to make a buttery syrup.

6 Loosen the edges of the puddings with a knife, then invert onto warmed serving plates. Pour a little sauce over each one and serve with cream or crème fraîche.

TOP TIP
The puddings can be frozen uncooked, for a later date. Bake as above, from frozen, allowing an extra 5 minutes cooking time.

VARIATIONS
- *Use chopped dates, dried figs or prunes instead of raisins.*
- *Replace the lemon in the sauce with orange rind and juice.*

FRUITY BREAD AND BUTTER PUDDING

Serves: 6
Preparation time: 20 minutes, plus soaking
Cooking time: 40 minutes
Freezing: not suitable
375 cals per serving

150g (5oz) dried fruit, such as apricots, prunes, figs and jumbo sultanas

45ml (3 tbsp) Grand Marnier

50g (2oz) unsalted butter

30ml (2 tbsp) marmalade

6 slices crusty white bread

grated rind of 1 orange

3 eggs

425ml (¾ pint) milk

50g (2oz) caster sugar

30–45ml (2–3 tbsp) runny honey, for drizzling

1 Roughly chop any large dried fruit, such as apricots, prunes and figs, then place with the rest of the fruit in a bowl and pour over the Grand Marnier. Leave to soak for 1 hour.

2 Preheat the oven to 180°C/350°F/gas 4. Butter an ovenproof dish and smear the chunky marmalade around the base and sides.

3 Butter the slices of bread and drain the fruit, keeping the soaking liquid on one side. Place the bread and fruit along with the orange rind in the prepared baking dish, distributing the fruit evenly by tucking the pieces in between the slices of bread.

4 In a bowl, whisk the eggs with the milk, sugar and the soaking liquid from the fruit and pour this mixture over the layers of fruit and bread. Leave to stand for 30 minutes.

5 Drizzle the honey over the pudding and bake in the preheated oven for 40 minutes or until browning and slightly set. Leave to stand for about 10 minutes, then serve.

TRADITIONAL APPLE PIE

Serves: 6
Preparation time: 35 minutes, plus
chilling
Cooking time: 30–40 minutes
Freezing: suitable
550 cals per serving

PASTRY
350g (12oz) plain white flour

pinch of salt

75g (3oz) butter, chilled and diced

75g (3oz) white vegetable fat,
chilled and diced

FILLING
700g (1½lb) cooking apples

finely grated rind and juice of
½ lemon

50g (2oz) granulated sugar

50g (2oz) dark soft brown sugar

15ml (1 tbsp) flour

pinch of freshly grated nutmeg

1.25ml (¼ tsp) ground cinnamon

finely grated rind and juice of
½ orange

50g (2oz) sultanas

15–25g (½–1oz) butter

TO FINISH
caster sugar, for sprinkling

1 First make the pastry. Mix the flour and salt together in a bowl. Add the butter and fat and, using your fingertips, rub them lightly into the flour until the mixture resembles fine breadcrumbs. Add 60–90ml (4–6 tbsp) chilled water, sprinkling it evenly over the surface. Stir in with a round-bladed knife until the mixture begins to stick together. With one hand, collect the dough mixture together to form a ball. Knead lightly for a few seconds to give a firm, smooth dough. Wrap in cling film and chill in the refrigerator for about 30 minutes.

2 Roll out two thirds of the pastry on a lightly floured work surface and use to line a 23cm (9 inch) pie dish. Chill in the refrigerator for 30 minutes, together with the remaining dough wrapped in cling film.

3 Meanwhile, to make the filling, peel, quarter and core the apples, then slice them thickly into a bowl of cold water to which the lemon juice has been added.

4 Preheat the oven to 190°C/375°F/gas 5. Mix the sugars, flour, nutmeg, cinnamon, lemon and orange rinds together and sprinkle a little of this onto the pastry lining.

5 Cover the base of the pastry lining with half the sliced apples, then sprinkle with half the sultanas and half the remaining sugar mixture. Repeat, using all the apples, sultanas and sugar. Sprinkle the fruit with the orange juice and dot with the butter.

6 Roll out the remaining pastry and use to cover the pie, sealing the edges well. Slash the top twice to let steam escape.

7 Cut leaves and berries from the pastry trimmings. Brush the top of the pie with water and position the decorations. Dredge with caster sugar. Bake in the preheated oven for 35–40 minutes until the fruit is tender and the top is golden brown. Serve with custard or cream.

APPLE BRAMBLE PUDDING

Serves: 6
Preparation time: 25 minutes
Cooking time: 25 minutes
Freezing: not suitable
430 cals per serving

125g (4oz) unsalted butter

75g (3oz) demerara sugar

700g (1½lb) cooking apples

30ml (2 tbsp) lemon juice

350g (12oz) blackberries

225g (8oz) raspberries

125g (4oz) red or blackcurrants

6 slices traditional white loaf

15ml (1 tbsp) oil

a little demerara sugar, for sprinkling

1 Preheat the oven to 200°C/400°F/gas 6. Lightly grease a 1.7 litre (3 pint) ovenproof dish. Melt 50g (2oz) of the butter in a large pan. Add the sugar and stir until beginning to dissolve.

2 Peel, core and thickly slice the apples and add to the pan. Cook gently, stirring frequently, for 5 minutes. Add the lemon juice, blackberries, raspberries and red or blackcurrants; toss lightly to combine.

3 Spoon half the fruit mixture into the base of the ovenproof dish. Remove the crusts from the bread if preferred. Melt the remaining butter in a frying pan with the oil, add half of the bread slices and fry until beginning to brown on the underside. Remove with a fish slice and lay the slices, browned sides uppermost, over the fruits in the dish. Reserve the butter and oil.

4 Spread the rest of the fruits and juices over the bread. Cut the remaining bread into triangles and arrange over the fruit in the dish. Brush liberally with the reserved butter and oil, then sprinkle with the demerara sugar. Bake in the oven for about 25 minutes until the bread topping is deep golden. Serve with custard or cream.

VARIATIONS
Virtually any combination of soft fruits can be used in this pudding, but avoid too many blackcurrants as their flavour will dominate.

TREACLE TART

Serves: 8–10

Preparation time: 25 minutes, plus chilling

Cooking time: 25–50 minutes

Freezing: suitable

620–495 cals per serving

PASTRY
225g (8oz) plain white flour

150g (5oz) unsalted butter

1 egg yolk

15g (½oz) caster sugar

FILLING
700g (1½lb) golden syrup

175g (6oz) white breadcrumbs

grated rind of 3 lemons

2 eggs

1 To make the pastry, sift the flour and put in a food processor. Add the butter, cut into small pieces, and work until the mixture resembles breadcrumbs. Add the egg yolk, sugar and about 30ml (2 tbsp) cold water; process briefly to a firm dough. Turn onto a lightly floured surface and knead lightly, then wrap in cling film and chill in the refrigerator for 30 minutes.

2 Preheat the oven to 180°C/350°F/gas 4. Roll out the pastry on a lightly floured surface and use to line a 25cm (10 inch) shallow fluted flan tin, about 4cm (1½ inches) deep. Trim off the excess pastry and flute the edges. Prick the base with a fork.

3 For the filling, lightly heat the golden syrup in a saucepan until thinned in consistency. Remove from the heat and mix with the breadcrumbs and lemon rind. Lightly beat the eggs and stir into the syrup mixture. Pour the filling into the pastry case.

4 Bake in the oven for about 45–50 minutes until the filling is lightly set and turning golden. Allow to cool slightly. Serve with crème fraîche or ice cream.

RICE PUDDING WITH SUMMER FRUIT COMPÔTE

Serves: 4
Preparation time: 10 minutes
Cooking time: 2 hours
Freezing: suitable (for compôte only)
495 cals per serving

25g (1oz) unsalted butter
50g (2oz) pudding rice
600ml (1 pint) milk
300ml (½ pint) double cream
15ml (1 tbsp) caster sugar
pinch of salt
freshly grated nutmeg

SUMMER FRUIT COMPÔTE
225g (8oz) strawberries
125g (4oz) blueberries
50g (2oz) caster sugar
grated rind and juice of 1 orange
150g (5oz) raspberries
85g (3oz) redcurrants
5ml (1 tsp) vanilla essence

1 Preheat the oven to 150°C/300°F/gas 2, then lightly butter an ovenproof dish using about half the butter.

2 Add the rice to the dish and pour in the milk and cream. Add the sugar and salt and stir. Dot the remaining butter on top and sprinkle with nutmeg. Place in the preheated oven and cook for 2 hours. During the cooking time stir the pudding 2 or 3 times to break up the skin forming on top.

3 About 10 minutes before the pudding is cooked, prepare the fruit compote. Hull the strawberries and place in a saucepan along with the blueberries, sugar, orange rind and juice. Heat gently until the berries begin to soften. Add the raspberries, redcurrants and vanilla essence and warm through gently.

4 When the rice pudding is ready, remove from the oven, sprinkle over a fine grating of nutmeg and serve alongside the fruit compôte. Both the pudding and compôte can be served hot or cold.

RATAFIA BAKEWELL TART

Serves: 8

Preparation time: 30 minutes, plus chilling

Cooking time: about 50 minutes

Freezing: suitable (without topping)

500 cals per serving

PASTRY

225g (8oz) plain white flour

50g (2oz) lightly salted butter

50g (2oz) white vegetable fat

FILLING

60ml (4 tbsp) apricot conserve or jam

50g (2oz) ratafia biscuits

75g (3oz) unsalted butter

3 eggs

125g (4oz) caster sugar

5ml (1 tsp) almond essence

125g (4oz) ground almonds

CARAMEL ORANGES

4 oranges

175g (6oz) sugar

600ml (1 pint) water

TO FINISH

icing sugar, for dusting

1 To make the pastry, sift the flour into a bowl. Add the fats, cut into small pieces, and rub in with the fingertips until the mixture resembles fine breadcrumbs. Stir in enough water to make a firm dough. Knead lightly, then wrap in cling film and chill for 30 minutes.

2 Preheat the oven to 200°C/400°F/gas 6. Preheat a baking sheet. Roll out the pastry on a lightly floured surface and use to line a 23cm (9 inch) spring-release cake tin. Spread the apricot conserve over the base. Halve the ratafia biscuits.

3 Melt the butter and set aside. Place the eggs and sugar in a large bowl and whisk until the mixture is thick enough for the whisk to leave a trail when lifted from the bowl. Pour in the melted butter around the edge of the bowl. Add the almond essence and scatter over the ground almonds and ratafia biscuits. Fold in carefully, using a large metal spoon, until just combined.

4 Turn the mixture into the pastry-lined tin. Place on the preheated baking sheet and bake for 10 minutes. Reduce the oven temperature to 180°C/350°F/gas 4 and bake for a further 40 minutes or until the filling is firm and set.

5 Meanwhile prepare the caramel oranges. Pare strips of rind from 1 orange. Peel the other 3 oranges, discarding all white pith, then slice thinly. Dissolve the sugar in the water in a heavy-based pan over a low heat. Increase heat and boil steadily for 5 minutes. Add the orange slices and rind strips. Bring to the boil, then simmer gently for 15 minutes. Remove the fruit and rind with a slotted spoon and cook the syrup for a further 20 minutes until pale golden. Return the fruit to the syrup.

6 When the tart has finished baking, arrange of the caramel oranges on top of the tart, spooning a little of the syrup over them. Allow the tart to cool slightly, then remove from the tin and place on a serving plate. Dust edges with icing sugar and serve warm or cold with cream or crème fraîche.

TOP TIP
Don't worry if the tart sinks slightly in the centre. This accentuates its lovely cracked crust.

INDIVIDUAL BLACKBERRY AND APPLE FLAPJACK PUDDINGS

Serves: 4–6
Preparation time: 10 minutes
Cooking time: 30 minutes
Freezing: suitable
455–305 cals per serving

2 large cooking apples

50g (2oz) sugar

100g (4oz) fresh blackberries

TOPPING
85g (3oz) unsalted butter

30ml (2 tbsp) golden syrup

25g (1oz) soft light brown sugar

125g (4oz) porridge oats

25g (1oz) dessicated coconut

1 Peel, core and chop the apples and put them in a saucepan. Add the sugar and sufficient water to start cooking the apples, about 30ml (2 tbsp). Place over a low heat, bring to simmering point and cook gently for 5 minutes. Stir in the blackberries and put aside to cool.

2 For the flapjack topping melt the butter, syrup and sugar in another saucepan and stir in the porridge oats and dessicated coconut.

3 Preheat the oven to 180°C/350°F/gas 4. Divide the blackberry and apple mixture into individual baking dishes and spoon over a layer of flapjack topping. Place the dishes on a baking tray and bake in the preheated oven for 20 minutes or until brown and bubbling. Allow to stand for 5 minutes before serving with vanilla ice cream.

ST CLEMENT'S PUDDING

Serves: 4
Preparation time: 15–20 minutes
Cooking time: about 45 minutes
Freezing: not suitable
335 cals per serving

50g (2oz) butter or margarine

125g (4oz) caster sugar

1 orange

2 small lemons

2 eggs, separated

50g (2oz) self-raising flour

300ml (½ pint) milk

1 Preheat the oven to 190°C/375°F/gas 5. Lightly grease a 1.1 litre (2 pint), deep ovenproof dish.

2 In a bowl, beat the butter with the sugar and the grated rinds of the orange and 1 lemon until pale and fluffy. Add the egg yolks and flour; beat well. Stir in the milk, 45ml (3 tbsp) strained lemon juice and 30ml (2 tbsp) strained orange juice.

3 Whisk the egg whites until they hold soft peaks, then fold into the mixture with a large metal spoon. Pour into the dish.

4 Stand the dish in a roasting tin containing enough water to come halfway up the side of the dish. Bake in the preheated oven for about 45 minutes or until spongy to the touch.

CINNAMON BREAD WITH STRAWBERRY COMPÔTE

Serves: 6
Preparation time: 20 minutes, plus soaking
Cooking time: about 10 minutes
Freezing: not suitable
430 cals per serving

STRAWBERRY COMPÔTE
450g (1lb) strawberries

25g (1oz) caster sugar

1 cinnamon stick, halved

45ml (3 tbsp) redcurrant jelly

squeeze of lemon juice, to taste

CINNAMON BREAD
6 thick slices white bread, about 2cm (¾ inch) thick

3 egg yolks

2.5ml (½ tsp) vanilla essence

65g (2½oz) caster sugar

150ml (¼ pint) double cream

50ml (2fl oz) milk

50g (2oz) unsalted butter

15ml (1 tbsp) oil

1.25ml (¼ tsp) ground cinnamon

TO DECORATE
fresh lemon balm or mint sprigs

1 To make the compôte, hull the strawberries and halve any large ones. Place in a saucepan with the sugar and cinnamon stick. Cover and heat very gently until the strawberries are beginning to soften.

2 Melt the redcurrant jelly in a separate saucepan with 15ml (1 tbsp) water. Pour over the strawberries. Stir lightly and remove from the heat. Add a little lemon juice to taste.

3 Cut a 7.5cm (3 inch) square from each bread slice. Cut each square in half diagonally to make triangles. Lightly beat the egg yolks with the vanilla essence, 15ml (1 tbsp) sugar, the cream and milk.

4 Place the bread slices in a single layer on two large plates. Pour the egg mixture over them and leave to stand for 10 minutes until absorbed.

5 Melt the butter with the oil in a large frying pan. Add half the bread triangles and fry for 2 minutes or until golden on the undersides. Turn the bread and fry for another 1 minute. Drain and keep warm while frying the remainder, adding a little more butter to the pan if necessary.

6 Mix the remaining sugar and cinnamon together and use to coat the fried bread. Arrange on serving plates with the strawberries and juice. Decorate with fresh lemon balm or mint sprigs.

TOP TIP
Use bread that's one or two days old if available, as it will be easier to cut and soak.

VARIATIONS
Use raspberries instead of the strawberries, heating them briefly in the melted redcurrant jelly, rather than softening them first. Lightly poached sweet plums or apricots would also work well.

APRICOT AND CARDAMOM MERINGUE PIE

Serves: 8
Preparation time: 20–25 minutes
Cooking time: 2 hours
Freezing: not suitable
405 cals per serving

225g (8oz) hobnob biscuits

125g (4oz) unsalted butter, melted

600g (1lb 5oz) fresh apricots

10ml (2 tsp) cardomom pods
(to give about 2.5ml (½ tsp) seeds)

45ml (3 tbsp) runny honey

4 eggs, separated, plus 2 egg yolks

pinch of salt

175g (6oz) caster sugar

15ml (1 tbsp) granulated sugar

1 Preheat the oven to 200°C/400°F/gas 6. Crush the hobnob biscuits into a bowl and stir in the melted butter. Push the crumbs into a 25cm (10 inch) fluted flan case, making sure the crumbs go up the sides of the dish. Bake in the preheated oven for 10 minutes. Remove from the oven and reduce the oven temperature to 180°C/350°F/gas 4.

2 Crush the cardomom pods, remove the seeds and crush these in a pestle and mortar. Halve and stone the apricots and place them in an ovenproof dish. Scatter over the crushed cardamom seeds, then pour over the honey. Cover the dish with foil and bake in the hot oven for 30–40 minutes or until the fruit is soft. Remove from the oven and reduce the oven temperature to 150°C/300°F/gas 2.

3 Allow the apricots to cool slightly and then place in a food processor or blender and process to form a purée. Stir in the egg yolks and pour this mixture into the prepared biscuit base. Place in the oven and cook until set, about 40 minutes. Remove from the oven and increase the oven temperature to 200°C/400°F/gas 6.

4 Whisk the egg whites with the salt until stiff and gradually add the caster sugar, whisking until the mixture forms stiff peaks. Spoon over the apricot filling in the pie, sprinkle with the granulated sugar and return to the oven for a further 15–20 minutes or until the meringue is golden brown and set. Serve warm or cold.

GOOSEBERRY FOOL

Serves: 4–6

Preparation time: 30 minutes, plus chilling

Cooking time: 10 minutes

Freezing: suitable

360–240 cals per serving

900g (2lb) fresh or frozen gooseberries

90–125g (3–4oz) caster sugar, to taste

15ml (1 tbsp) powdered gelatine

150ml (¼ pint) double cream

fresh mint sprigs or lemon geranium leaves, to decorate

1 Top and tail the gooseberries and place in a saucepan with the sugar and 60ml (4 tbsp) water. Cover tightly and simmer gently for about 10 minutes until the fruit is soft and pulpy. Cool slightly, then press the fruit through a nylon sieve to remove the pips; there should be about 800ml (1½ pints) of purée.

2 Spoon 45ml (3 tbsp) water into a small bowl. Sprinkle over the gelatine and leave to soak for 2–3 minutes or until sponge-like. Stand the bowl over a pan of gently simmering water for 2–3 minutes until the gelatine is dissolved. Stir into the gooseberry purée and cool.

3 Whip the double cream until it just holds its shape – it should be of a similar consistency to the gooseberry purée. Gently fold the cream into the cold gooseberry purée.

4 Spoon into serving glasses, cover and chill in the refrigerator for about 2 hours until set. Decorate with mint or lemon geranium leaves to serve.

VARIATIONS
- *Apricot and Ginger Fool: replace the gooseberries with apricots and add a little finely chopped stem ginger.*
- *Pear and Cinnamon Fool: replace the stewed gooseberries with poached pears. Sweeten the puréed pears with brown sugar and a pinch of ground cinnamon to taste.*

SHERRY TRIFLE WITH SOFT FRUITS

Serves: 10

Preparation time: 45 minutes, plus cooling

Cooking time: 40 minutes

Freezing: not suitable

660 cals per serving

SPONGE

125g (4oz) self-raising flour

1.25ml (¼ tsp) baking powder

75g (3oz) unsalted butter, softened

75g (3oz) caster sugar

2 eggs

grated rind of 1 orange or lemon

CUSTARD

4 egg yolks

15ml (1 tbsp) cornflour

5ml (1 tsp) vanilla essence

125g (4oz) caster sugar

600ml (1 pint) milk

TO FINISH

60ml (1½lb) mixed soft fruits, such as raspberries, redcurrants and blackberries

100ml (3½fl oz) sherry

90ml (3fl oz) freshly squeezed orange juice

750ml (1¼ pints) double cream

15ml (1 tbsp) icing sugar

30ml (2 tbsp) brandy

finely grated rind of 1 orange

soft fruits and fresh mint sprigs, to decorate

1 To make the sponge, grease and line an 18cm (7 inch) cake tin with greaseproof paper. Preheat the oven to 180°C/350°F/gas 4. Sift the flour and baking powder into a bowl. Add the butter, sugar, eggs and orange or lemon rind and beat using an electric whisk until pale and creamy. Turn into the prepared tin and bake for about 40 minutes until risen and just firm to the touch. Leave to cool.

2 For the custard, in a bowl whisk the egg yolks, cornflour, vanilla and caster sugar with a little of the milk. Bring the remaining milk to the boil in a saucepan, then pour over the egg mixture, whisking constantly. Return to the saucepan and cook gently, stirring, until thickened enough to coat the back of the spoon; do not boil.

3 Turn the custard into a bowl and cover the surface with greaseproof paper to prevent a skin forming. Leave to cool completely.

4 Split the sponge and sandwich with the raspberry conserve. Cut into pieces and scatter into a glass serving dish. Scatter the fruit over the sponge.

5 Mix together the sherry and orange juice and pour over the fruits and sponge. Cover with the custard.

6 Whip the cream in a bowl with the icing sugar, brandy and orange rind until just peaking. Spread over the custard.

7 Serve decorated with soft fruits and fresh mint sprigs.

TOP TIP

If you haven't time to make your own sponge, use 350g (12oz) bought Madeira cake instead.

CLOTTED CREAM ICE CREAM

Serves: 4–6

Preparation time: 20 minutes, plus freezing

Cooking time: about 10 minutes

425 cals per serving

125g (4oz) caster sugar

3 egg yolks

10ml (2 tsp) cornflour

2.5ml (½ tsp) vanilla essence

150ml (¼ pint) double cream

400g (14oz) clotted cream

ripe soft fruits, such as raspberries and strawberries, to serve

1 Set the freezer to fast-freeze. Put the sugar in a saucepan with 150ml (¼ pint) water and heat gently, stirring until dissolved. Bring to the boil and boil for 1 minute. Remove from the heat and allow the syrup to cool slightly.

2 Put the egg yolks, cornflour and vanilla essence in a bowl with half of the double cream. Beat until smooth. Heat the remaining double cream in a saucepan with the clotted cream until almost boiling. Pour over the egg yolk mixture, stirring.

3 Return to the saucepan and heat gently, stirring until slightly thickened. Leave to cool, then stir in the syrup.

4 Transfer the ice cream to an ice cream maker and follow the manufacturer's instructions. Then transfer to a freezerproof container and place in the freezer until ready to serve or freeze in a freezerproof container until semi-frozen, then whisk lightly to break up the ice crystals and return to the freezer until firm.

5 Transfer the ice cream to the refrigerator about 30 minutes before serving to soften slightly. Serve scooped into individual dishes with soft fruits.

VARIATIONS

• Soft fruit ice cream: purée 350g (12oz) mixed ripe strawberries, raspberries and redcurrants in a blender or food processor, then sieve to remove the pips. Stir into the cream before freezing.

• Almond and amaretto ice cream: reduce the caster sugar to 50g (2oz). Stir in 75g (3oz) crushed macaroon biscuits and 30ml (2 tbsp) amaretto liqueur after whisking the partially frozen ice cream.

• Creamy fudge ice cream: reduce the caster sugar to 25g (1oz). Grate 75g (3oz) cream fudge and stir in after whisking the partially frozen ice cream.

• Pear and ginger ice cream: soak 75g (3oz) dried pears in cold water overnight. Drain, chop and add to the sugar syrup. Finely chop 15g (½oz) preserved stem ginger and add with the pears after whisking the partially frozen ice cream.

BAKED PLUMS AND STEM GINGER WITH CINNAMON CREAM

Serves: 6
Preparation time: 10 minutes
Cooking time: 20 minutes
Freezing: suitable
370 cals per serving

10–12 ripe plums

2 pieces of preserved ginger, plus 15ml (1 tbsp) of ginger preserving syrup

85g (3oz) unsalted butter

finely grated rind of 1 lemon

30–45ml (2–3 tbsp) demerara sugar

CINNAMON CREAM
225g (8oz) mascarpone cheese

a little milk to soften

1.25ml (¼ tsp) ground cinnamon

2.5ml (½ tsp) caster sugar

1 Preheat the oven to 200°C/400°F/gas 6. Halve and stone the plums and place in an ovenproof dish.

2 Finely chop the preserved ginger. In a small saucepan melt the butter with the lemon rind, chopped ginger and the ginger syrup and spoon over the plums. Place in the oven for 20 minutes or until the edges of the plums are slightly browned.

3 Meanwhile make the cinnamon cream. Soften the mascarpone cheese with a little milk, then stir in the ground cinnamon and caster sugar.

4 When the plums are baked, remove from the oven, scatter with demerara sugar and serve warm with the cinnamon cream.

CHOCOLATE CRÈME BRÛLÉE

Serves: 6–8

Preparation time: 15 minutes, plus infusing

Cooking time: 20 minutes, plus overnight chilling

Freezing: not suitable

500–380 cals per serving

450ml (¾ pint) double cream

60ml (4 tbsp) milk

1 vanilla pod, split

6 egg yolks

50g (2oz) caster sugar

75g (3oz) good-quality plain chocolate

demerara sugar, for sprinkling

1 Pour the cream and milk into a saucepan. Scrape the vanilla seeds into the cream, adding the pod as well. Bring slowly to the boil, then turn off the heat and leave to infuse for 15 minutes.

2 Whisk the egg yolks and sugar together in a bowl until pale and creamy. Place the chocolate in a food processor or blender and process to break it up. Remove the vanilla pod from the cream.

3 With the motor running, pour the hot cream into the food processor and whizz until the chocolate is melted and the mixture is smooth. Pour this over the whisked egg and sugar mixture and stir well. Return to the saucepan and stir with a wooden spoon over a low heat for about 20 minutes until thickened; do not allow to boil or it will curdle.

4 Strain the mixture into a jug, then pour into the ramekins, filling them to the top; the custard will sink as it cools. Do not cover, but cool completely. Chill overnight to set.

5 Preheat the grill to its hottest setting. Sprinkle a very thin even layer of sugar over the surface of each custard; it should be about one sugar grain thick. Set the ramekins on a sturdy baking tray and place under the grill as close to the element as possible. Watch carefully and remove as soon as the sugar caramelises. Leave to cool completely, then chill again before serving.

VARIATION
Add 15ml (1 tbsp) good-quality instant coffee to the cream for a mocha flavour.

STICKY CHOCOLATE BROWNIES WITH PRUNES

Serves: 6–8
Preparation: 15 minutes
Cooking time: 50 minutes
Freezing: suitable
460–345 cals per serving

25g (1oz) whole blanched almonds

coffee for soaking the prunes

85g (3oz) pitted prunes

50g (2oz) good-quality plain chocolate

125g (4oz) unsalted butter, cut into small pieces

2 medium eggs

225g (8oz) granulated sugar

50g (2oz) self-raising flour

1.25ml (¼ tsp) salt

icing sugar, for dusting

1 Line the base and the sides of a 20cm (8 inch) round cake tin with baking parchment. Preheat the oven to 180°C/350°F/gas 4.

2 Lightly toast the almonds, and when cool roughly chop.

3 Prepare some fresh strong coffee, and while it is still hot pour it over the prunes to cover them. Put aside for 30 minutes.

4 Meanwhile, put the chocolate and butter into a large bowl placed on top of a saucepan filled with water. Bring the water to the boil and continue to boil very gently until the chocolate has melted. Remove the bowl carefully from the saucepan and add the eggs, sugar, flour, salt and chopped almonds. Remove the prunes from their soaking liquid and stir them into the mixture. Pour the mixture into the prepared tin and place in the hot oven for 45 minutes.

5 Remove from the oven and leave to cool in the tin for 10 minutes before cutting and dusting with icing sugar. Serve slightly warm, preferably with cream or vanilla ice cream.

GLOSSARY

A brief guide to cooking methods, terms and ingredients used in the recipes featured in this book.

ACIDULATED WATER Water to which lemon juice or vinegar has been added in which fruit or vegetables, such as pears or Jerusalem artichokes, are immersed to prevent discoloration.

AL DENTE Italian term used to describe food, especially pasta and vegetables, which is cooked until tender but still firm to the bite.

ANTIPASTO Italian selection of cold meats, fish, salads etc. served as a starter.

ARROWROOT Fine, white powder used as a thickening agent for sauces. Unlike cornflour, arrowroot gives a clear gloss.

AU GRATIN Describes a dish which has been coated with sauce, sprinkled with breadcrumbs or cheese and browned under the grill or in the oven. Low-sided gratin dishes are used.

BAIN-MARIE Literally, a water bath, used to keep foods, such as delicate custards and sauces, at a constant low temperature during cooking. On the hob a double saucepan or bowl over a pan of simmering water is used; for oven cooking, the baking dish(es) is placed in a roasting tin containing enough hot water to come halfway up the sides.

BAKING BLIND Pre-baking a pastry case before filling. The pastry case is lined with greaseproof paper and weighted down with dried beans or ceramic baking beans.

BAKING POWDER A raising agent consisting of an acid, usually cream of tartar and an alkali, such as bicarbonate of soda, which react to produce carbon dioxide. This expands during baking and makes cakes and breads rise.

BALSAMIC VINEGAR Italian oak-aged vinegar, dark brown in colour with a superior sweet, mellow flavour.

BARD To cover the breast of game birds, poultry or lean meat with fat to prevent the meat from drying out during roasting.

BASTE To spoon the juices and melted fat over meat, poultry, game or vegetables during roasting to keep them moist. The term is also used to describe spooning over a marinade.

BEAT Method of incorporating air into an ingredient or mixture by agitating it vigorously with a spoon, fork, whisk or electric mixer. Also used to soften ingredients.

BÉCHAMEL Classic French white sauce, used as the basis for other sauces and savoury dishes.

BEURRE MANIÉ Equal parts of flour and butter kneaded together to form a paste. Used for thickening soups, stews and casseroles. It is whisked into the hot liquid a little at a time at the end of cooking.

BIND To mix beaten egg or other liquid into a dry mixture to hold it together.

BLANCH To immerse food, such as tomatoes, briefly in fast-boiling water to loosen skins, to remove bitterness, or to destroy enzymes and preserve the colour, flavour and texture of vegetables (especially prior to freezing).

BONE To remove the bones from meat, poultry, game or fish, so it can be stuffed or simply rolled before cooking.

BOUQUET GARNI Small bunch of herbs – usually a mixture of parsley stems, thyme and a bay leaf – tied in muslin and used to flavour stocks, soups and stews.

BRAISE To cook meat, poultry, game or vegetables slowly in a small amount of liquid in a pan or casserole with a tight-fitting lid. The food is usually browned first in oil.

BROCHETTE Food cooked on a skewer or spit.

BRÛLÉE A French term, literally meaning 'burnt', used to refer to a dish with a crisp coating of caramelised sugar.

BUTTERFLY To split a food, such as a large prawn or poussin, almost in half and open out flat, so that it will cook more quickly.

CALORIE Strictly a kilocalorie, this is used in dietetics to measure the energy value of foods.

CANAPÉ Small appetiser, usually consisting of a pastry or bread base with a savoury topping, served with drinks.

CAPER Small bud of a Mediterranean flowering shrub, usually packed in brine. Small French capers in balsamic vinegar are considered to be the best.

CARAMELISE To heat sugar or sugar syrup slowly until it is brown in colour; ie forms a caramel.

CARBONADE Rich meat braise which includes beer.

CASSEROLE Strictly speaking, a dish with a tight-fitting lid used for slow-cooking meat, poultry and vegetables. Now applied to the food cooked in this way.

CHARCUTERIE French term for cooked pork products, including hams, sausages and terrines.

CHILL To cool food in the refrigerator.

CHINE To sever the rib bones from the backbone, close to the spine. This is done to meat joints, such as loin of pork or lamb, to make them easier to carve into chops after cooking.

CLARIFY To remove sediment or impurities from a liquid. Stock is clarified by heating with egg white, while butter is clarified by melting and skimming. Butter which is clarified will withstand a higher frying temperature. To clarify butter: Heat until melted and all bubbling stops. Remove from the heat and let stand until the sediment has sunk to the bottom, then gently pour off the fat, straining it through muslin.

COCONUT MILK Used in curries and other ethnic dishes. Available in cans from larger supermarkets and ethnic stores. Alternatively creamed coconut sold compressed in blocks can be reconstituted to make coconut milk.

COMPÔTE Mixture of fresh or dried fruit stewed in sugar syrup. Served hot or cold.

CONCASSÉ Diced fresh ingredient, used as a garnish. The term is most often applied to skinned, seeded tomatoes.

COULIS A smooth fruit or vegetable purée, thinned if necessary to a pouring consistency.

COURT BOUILLON Aromatic cooking liquid containing wine, vinegar or lemon juice, used for poaching delicate fish, poultry or vegetables.

CONSISTENCY Term used to describe the texture of a mixture, eg firm, dropping or soft.

CREAM OF TARTAR Also known as tartaric acid, this is a raising agent which is also an ingredient of baking powder and self-raising flour.

CREAM To beat together fat and sugar until the mixture is pale and fluffy, and resembles whipped cream in texture and colour. The method is used in cakes and puddings which contain a high proportion of fat and require the incorporation of a lot of air.

CRÊPE French term for a pancake.

CRIMP To decorate the edge of a pie, tart or shortbread by pinching it at regular intervals to give a fluted effect.

CROQUETTE Seasoned mixture of cooked potato and fish, meat, poultry or vegetables shaped into a small roll, coated with egg and breadcrumbs and shallow-fried.

CROÛTE Circle or other shaped piece of fried bread, typically used as a base for serving small game birds.

CROÛTONS Small pieces of fried or toasted bread, served with soups and salads.

CRUDITÉS Raw vegetables, usually cut into slices or sticks, typically served with a dip or sauce as an appetiser.

CRYSTALLISE To preserve fruit in sugar syrup.

CURDS The part of milk which coagulates when natural fermentation takes place or when a curdling agent, such as rennet, is added.

CURDLE To cause sauces or creamed mixtures to separate once the egg is added, usually by overheating or over-beating.

CURE To preserve fish, meat or poultry by smoking, drying or salting.

DARIOLE Small, narrow mould with sloping sides used to make individual puddings.

DAUBE Braising meat and vegetables with stock, often with wine and herbs added.

DEGLAZE To heat stock, wine or other liquid with the cooking juices left in the pan after roasting or sautéing, scraping and stirring vigorously to dissolve the sediment on the base of the pan.

DÉGORGE To draw out moisture from a food, eg salting aubergines to remove bitter juices.

DICE To cut food into small cubes.

DRAW To remove the entrails from poultry or game.

DREDGE To sprinkle food generously with flour, sugar, icing sugar etc.

DRESS To pluck, draw and truss poultry or game. The term is also used to describe tossing a salad in vinaigrette or other dressing.

DRIPPING Fat obtained from roasting meat.

DROPPING CONSISTENCY Term used to describe the required texture of a cake or pudding mixture just before cooking. Test for it by taking a spoonful of the mixture and holding the spoon on its side above the bowl. The mixture should fall of its own accord within 5 seconds.

DRY To preserve food by dehydration. Rice, pasta, pulses and dried fruit are treated in this way.

DUST To sprinkle lightly with flour, cornflour, icing sugar etc.

EMULSION A mixture of two liquids which do not dissolve into one another, eg oil and vinegar. Vigorous shaking, whisking or heating will emulsify them, as in a vinaigrette.

EN CROÛTE Term used to describe food which is wrapped in pastry before cooking.

EN PAPILLOTE Term used to describe food which is baked in a greaseproof paper or baking parchment parcel and served from the paper.

ENZYME Organic substance in food which causes chemical changes. Enzymes are a complex group. Their action is usually halted during cooking.

ESCALOPE Thin slice of meat, such as pork, veal or turkey, cut from the top of the leg, usually pan-fried.

EXTRACT Concentrated flavouring which is used in small quantities, eg yeast extract, vanilla extract.

FERMENT Chemical change deliberately or accidentally brought about by fermenting agents, such as yeast or bacteria. Fermentation is utilised for making bread, yogurt, beer and wine.

FILLET Term used to describe boned breasts of birds, boned sides of fish, and the undercut of a loin of beef, lamb, pork or veal.

FILO PASTRY A popular type of Greek pastry manufactured in wafer-thin sheets and sold in packets or boxes. It must be kept covered to prevent it drying out.

FINES HERBES Classic French mixture of chopped herbs, ie parsley, tarragon, chives and chervil.

FLAKE To separate food, such as cooked fish, into natural pieces.

FLAMBÉ Flavouring a dish with alcohol, usually brandy or rum, which is then ignited so that the actual alcohol content is burned off.

FOLDING IN Method of combining a whisked or creamed mixture with other ingredients by cutting and folding so that it retains its lightness. A large metal spoon or plastic bladed spatula is used.

FROSTING To coat leaves and flowers with a fine layer of sugar to use as a decoration. Also an American term for icing cakes.

FRY To cook food in hot fat or oil. There are various methods: shallow-frying in a little fat in a shallow pan, deep-frying where the food is totally immersed in oil, dry-frying in which fatty foods are cooked in a non-stick pan without extra fat; see also Stir-frying.

GALETTE Cooked savoury or sweet mixture shaped into a round.

GARNISH A decoration, usually edible, such as parsley or lemon, which is used to enhance the appearance of a savoury dish.

GELATINE An animal-derived gelling agent sold in powdered form, and as leaf gelatine. Used in jellies, mousses and cold soufflés.

GELAZONE A vegetarian gelling agent sold in powdered form in sachets, and used as a substitute for gelatine.

GHEE Clarified butter widely used in Indian cookery.

GLAZE A glossy coating given to sweet and savoury dishes to improve their appearance and sometimes flavour. Ingredients for glazes include beaten egg, egg white, milk and syrup.

GLUTEN A protein constituent of grains, such as wheat and rye, which develops when the flour is mixed with water to give the dough elasticity.

GRATE To shred hard food, such as cheese and carrots, with a grater or food processor attachment.

GRIDDLE A flat, heavy, metal plate used on the hob for cooking scones or for searing savoury ingredients.

GRIND To reduce foods such as coffee beans, nuts and spices to small particles using a food mill, pestle and mortar, electric grinder or food processor.

GUT To clean out the entrails from fish.

HANG To suspend meat or game in a cool, dry place for a number of days to tenderise the flesh and develop flavour.

HULL To remove the stalk and calyx from soft fruits, such as strawberries.

INFUSE To immerse flavourings, such as aromatic vegetables, herbs, spices and vanilla, in a liquid to impart flavour. Usually the infused liquid is brought to the boil, then left to stand for a while.

JULIENNE Fine matchstick strips of vegetables or citrus zest, sometimes used as a garnish.

KNEAD To work dough by pummelling with the heel of the hand.

KNOCK BACK To knead a yeast dough for a second time after rising, to ensure an even texture.

LARD To insert small strips of fat or streaky bacon into the flesh of game birds and dry meat before cooking. A special larding needle is used.

LIAISON A thickening or binding agent based on a combination of ingredients, such as flour and water or oil and egg.

MACERATE To soften and flavour raw or dried foods by soaking in a liquid, eg soaking fruit in alcohol.

MANDOLIN(E) A flat wooden or metal frame with adjustable cutting blades for cutting vegetables.

MARINATE To soak raw meat, poultry or game – usually in a mixture of oil, wine, vinegar and flavourings (a marinade) – to soften and impart flavour. The marinade may also be used to baste the food during cooking.

MEDALLION Small round piece of meat, usually beef or veal.

MINCE To cut food into very fine pieces, using a mincer, food processor or knife.

MOCHA Term which has come to mean a blend of chocolate and coffee.

PARBOIL To boil a vegetable or other food for part of its cooking time before finishing it by another method.

PARE To finely peel the skin or zest from vegetables or fruit.

PASSATA A purée of plum tomatoes, used in many Italian dishes. Available ready-made from supermarkets.

PÂTE The French word for pastry, familiar in pâte sucrée, a sweet flan pastry.

PÂTÉ A savoury mixture of finely chopped or minced meat, fish and/or vegetables, usually served as a starter with bread or toast and crudités.

PATTY TIN Tray of cup-shaped moulds for cooking small cakes and deep tartlets. Also called a bun tin.

PESTLE AND MORTAR Heavy marble or porcelain bowl with a heavy grinding tool for grinding herbs, spices etc.

PESTO A paste-like sauce made from puréed herbs and oil, used to flavour pasta and vegetables. A classic pesto is made from basil, pine nuts, garlic and olive oil.

PITH The bitter white skin under the thin zest of

citrus fruit.

PIZZA STONE A clay stone for pizza-baking which reproduces the intense heat of a professional pizza oven.

PLUCK To remove the feathers from poultry and game.

POACH To cook food gently in liquid at simmering point, so that the surface of the liquid is just trembling.

PROVE To leave bread dough to rise after shaping.

PURÉE To pound, sieve or liquidise fruit, vegetables or fish to a smooth pulp. Purées often form the basis for soups and sauces.

QUENELLES Fish, meat or poultry which has been blended to a fine paste, shaped into ovals, then poached in a liquid.

REDUCE To fast-boil stock or other liquid in an uncovered pan to evaporate water and concentrate the flavour.

REFRESH To cool hot vegetables very quickly by plunging them into ice-cold water or holding them under running water in order to stop the cooking process and preserve the colour.

RENDER To melt fat slowly to a liquid by heating meat trimmings, or to release the fat from fatty meat, such as duck or goose, during roasting.

ROAST To cook meat by dry heat in the oven.

ROULADE Soufflé or sponge mixture rolled around a savoury or sweet filling.

ROUX A mixture of equal quantities of butter (or other fat) and flour cooked together to form the basis of many sauces.

RUB IN Method of incorporating fat into flour by rubbing between the fingertips, used when a short texture is required. Used for pastry, cakes, scones and biscuits.

SALSA Piquant sauce made from chopped fresh vegetables and sometimes fruit.

SAUTÉ To cook food in a small quantity of fat over a high heat, shaking the pan constantly – usually in a sauté pan (a frying pan with straight sides and a wide base).

SCALD To pour boiling water over food to clean it, or loosen skin, eg tomatoes. Also used to describe heating milk to just below boiling point.

SCORE To cut parallel lines in the surface of food to improve its appearance or help it cook more quickly.

SEAR To brown meat quickly in a little hot fat before grilling or roasting.

SEASONED FLOUR Flour mixed with a little salt and pepper, used for dusting meat, fish etc before frying.

SHRED To grate cheese or slice vegetables into very fine pieces or strips.

SIEVE To press food through a perforated sieve to obtain a smooth texture.

SIFT To shake dry ingredients through a sieve to remove lumps.

SIMMER To keep a liquid just below boiling point.

SKIM To remove froth, scum or fat from the surface of stock, gravy, stews, jam etc. Use either a skimmer, a spoon or absorbent kitchen paper.

SPRING-RELEASE CAKE TIN Also known as a springform pan, this is a round cake tin with a spring-release side and removable base which is clamped in. Used for cakes and desserts which are not to be inverted.

STEAM To cook food in the steam of rapidly boiling water.

STEEP To immerse food in warm or cold liquid to soften it, and sometimes to draw out strong flavours.

STERILISE To destroy bacteria in foods by heating.

STEW To cook food, such as tougher cuts of meat, slowly in flavoured liquid which is kept at simmering point.

STIR-FRY To cook small even-sized pieces of food rapidly in a little fat, tossing it constantly over a high heat, usually in a wok.

SUET Hard fat of animal origin used in pastry and steamed puddings. A vegetarian alternative is available.

SUGAR SYRUP A concentrated solution of sugar in water used to make sorbets, granitas, fruit juices etc.

SWEAT To cook chopped or sliced vegetables in a little fat without liquid in a covered pan over a low heat.

SWISS ROLL TIN Shallow, rectangular tin, available in several different sizes, used for baking sponges which are filled and rolled after baking – such as roulades.

TEPID The term used to describe temperature at approximately blood heat, ie 37°C (98.7°F).

THERMOMETER, SUGAR/FAT Used for checking the temperature of boiling sugar syrups, and fat for deep-frying. Dual purpose thermometers are obtainable.

TRUSS To tie or skewer poultry or game into shape prior to roasting.

UNLEAVENED Made without a raising agent.

VANILLA SUGAR Sugar in which a vanilla pod has been stored to impart flavour.

WHIPPING (WHISKING) Beating air rapidly into a mixture either with a manual or electric whisk.

WOK Large Chinese pan with a rounded base and sloping sides, used for stir-frying.

ZEST The thin coloured outer layer of citrus fruit which contains essential oil.

ZESTER Small bevelled tool with five holes, drawn across citrus fruit to remove the zest in fine strips.

INDEX

ALSO IN THIS SERIES

LOW-FAT
COOKING
ISBN 0 09 187882 9
£9.99

QUICK & EASY
COOKING
ISBN 0 09 187885 3
£9.99

WORLD CLASSIC
COOKING
ISBN 0 09 187883 7
£9.99

AVAILABLE EXCLUSIVELY FROM WHSMITH